TOP 10
SAN DIEGO

PAMELA BARRUS

Top 10 San Diego Highlights

The Top 10 of Everything

CONTENTS

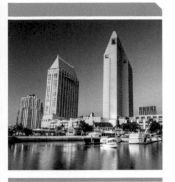

San Diego Area by Area

Streetsmart

The information in this DK Eyewitness Top 10 Travel Guide is checked regularly. Every effort has been made to ensure that this book is as up-to-date as possible at the time of going to press. Some details, however, such as telephone numbers, opening hours, prices, gallery hanging arrangements and travel information, are liable to change. The publishers cannot accept responsibility for any consequences arising from the use of this book, nor for any material on third party websites, and cannot guarantee that any website address in this book will be a suitable source of travel information. We value the views and suggestions of our readers very highly. Please write to: Publisher, DK Eyewitness Travel Guides, Dorling Kindersley, 80 Strand, London WC2R 0RL, Great Britain, or email travelguides@dk.com

Welcome to
San Diego

San Diego is the riviera of North America, pure and simple, with long stretches of spectacular sandy beaches. The birthplace of the state of California is also historic, hip, active, and friendly, bestowing a warm welcome upon visitors of all ages and every persuasion. With Eyewitness Top 10 San Diego, it's yours to explore.

San Diego boasts ritzy villages, retro surf towns, and movie-star good looks, with a cornucopia of gasp-worthy views, from the colorful flotilla of **San Diego Bay**, to the lush city of **La Jolla** to the north, and even parts of Mexico to the south. It is also one of the few places on earth where you can flit from ocean to mountains to desert and back to the city in the span of an afternoon. It is easy to see why San Diegans are proud of **Balboa Park**, with its showcase gardens, museums, and the famed **San Diego Zoo**. This is where locals keep fit, laze, dream, and play. And they do love to play, enjoying Comic-Con International, as well as festivals and outdoor concerts.

The city has all the advantages of a big city, minus the bustle, and a mild climate year-round. A stroll along the **Embarcadero** takes you from the historic *Star of India* tall ship, past the modern cruise terminal, all the way to the formidable **USS *Midway*** aircraft carrier. The historic **Gaslamp Quarter**, once home to bawdy houses, dance halls, and gambling saloons, is now full of popular shops, bars, and nightclubs. A number of original buildings have become superstar hotels and restaurants.

Whether you're visiting for a weekend or a week, our Top 10 guide outlines the best of everything San Diego offers. There are tips throughout, from seeking out what's free to avoiding the crowds, plus six easy-to-follow itineraries designed to tie together a clutch of sights in a short space of time. Add inspiring photography and easy-to-use maps, and you've got the essential pocket-sized travel companion. **Enjoy the book, and enjoy San Diego**.

Clockwise from top: **Spanish Village Art Center, Balboa Park; Scripps Pier, La Jolla; La Jolla Cove; exterior of the Mormon Temple; giant panda at the San Diego Zoo; marina with a view of downtown San Diego; the Prado at Balboa Park**

Exploring San Diego

A San Diego visit can hop from historic sights to sunny beaches to snowcapped mountains to exotic desert – and then back downtown in time for dinner. There is a wealth of things to see and do, and the city caters to every appetite and ability. These two- and four-day itineraries will help you plan your time and make the most of your visit to the city.

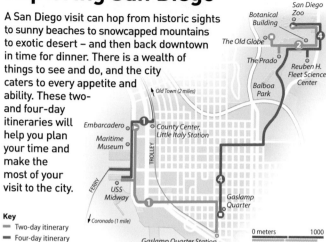

Key
— Two-day itinerary
— Four-day itinerary

Two Days in San Diego

Day ❶
MORNING
Awaken to a view of the bay and then take a morning stroll along the **Embarcadero** *(see pp14–15)*. Check out the vessels at the **Maritime Museum** *(see p47)*, and board the behemoth **USS** *Midway* *(see pp16–17)*.
AFTERNOON
Wander the historic **Gaslamp Quarter** *(see pp12–13)* on a self-guided or organized tour, then trolley to the **Old Town State Historic Park** *(see pp26–7)* and immerse yourself in early Californian life. Cap off the day at the **Mission Basilica San Diego de Alcalá** *(see pp32–3)*, before heading back to the coast to watch the sun set.

Day ❷
MORNING
Start off at the **San Diego Zoo** *(see pp20–21)*, touring by foot or tram, then explore the rest of **Balboa Park** *(see pp18–19)*. Browse Spanish Village artisan shops along the way.
AFTERNOON
Visit one or more of San Diego's renowned museums and galleries

(see p46–7); many of them have cafés for lunch. Rest your feet at the **Botanical Building** *(see p18)* and lily pond, where buskers perform nearby. Make advance reservations for dinner at **The Prado at Balboa Park** *(see pp64–5)*, and catch a show at **The Old Globe** *(see p60)*.

Four Days in San Diego

Day ❶
MORNING
Begin your day at **Old Town State Historic Park** *(see pp26–7)*, venturing out of the park to **Whaley House Museum** and **Presidio Park** *(see pp86–7)*. Shop for trinkets at **Bazaar del Mundo** *(see p88)*, then lunch at **Old Town Mexican Café & Cantina** *(see p89)*.
AFTERNOON
Trolley to the **Mission Basilica San Diego de Alcalá** *(see pp32–3)*, then head to the **Embarcadero** *(see pp14–15)*. Soak up the city's nautical heritage at the **Maritime Museum** *(see p47)* or **USS** *Midway* *(see pp16–17)*. Catch the ferry to **Coronado** *(see pp28–9)* for sunset cocktails at the **Hotel del Coronado** *(see p48)*.

Embarcadero, the waterfront area, has been the heart of San Diego since the mid-1500s.

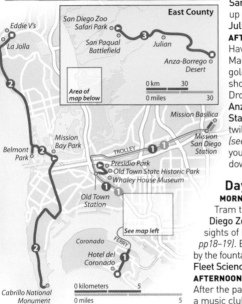

Day ❸
MORNING
Head northeast to **San Diego Zoo Safari Park** *(see p59)*. Continue past **San Pasqual Battlefield** up the mountain to **Julian** *(see pp44–5)*.
AFTERNOON
Have lunch on Julian's Main Street, pan for gold at Eagle Mine, and shop for local crafts. Drop down into the **Anza-Borrego Desert State Park** *(see p39)* at twilight. Indian casinos *(see p56)* may tempt you on the way back to downtown San Diego.

Day ❹
MORNING
Tram through the **San Diego Zoo** and head for the sights of **Balboa Park** *(see pp18–19)*. Enjoy a picnic lunch by the fountain outside **Reuben H. Fleet Science Center** *(see p59)*.
AFTERNOON
After the park, enjoy dinner and a music club in the historic **Gaslamp Quarter** *(see pp12–13)*, ending the day in the lively bars.

Day ❷
MORNING
Lazy beaches and lots of water- and land-based sports await visitors at **Mission Bay Park** *(see pp34–5)*. Take a spin on the 1925 Giant Dipper roller coaster at **Belmont Park** *(see p35)*.
AFTERNOON
Journey to the **Cabrillo National Monument** *(see p82)*. Explore tide pools and the lighthouse, and gaze over the busy bay from the visitor center. Continue up the coast to **La Jolla** *(see pp36–7)* to enjoy its chic shops, classy restaurants, and illustrious beaches. See the sun set over La Jolla Cove from **Eddie V's** upstairs patio, with live jazz *(see p65)*.

The Gaslamp Quarter is the most vibrant of San Diego's neighborhoods, with a great deal to see and do.

Top 10 San Diego Highlights

The idyllic beach at the waterfront area of Embarcadero

TOP 10 San Diego Highlights

With a sunny climate and a splendid setting along the Pacific, San Diegans live the California Dream. A vibrant downtown area and world-class attractions keep the city's spirit young, but its heart lies in its beginnings as the birthplace of California.

1 Gaslamp Quarter

Old wrought-iron gas lamps lead the way to the hottest scene in town. Rocking nightspots and vibrant restaurants give life to San Diego's historic downtown area (see pp12–13).

2 Embarcadero

With its nautical museums, vintage ships, and superb views across the harbor, the Embarcadero links the city to its ocean heritage (see pp14–17).

3 Balboa Park

San Diegans take pride in having one of the finest urban parks in the world. Its famous zoo, fascinating museums, and exquisite gardens offer endless activities (see pp18–23).

4 Old Town State Historic Park

In this, the original center of San Diego, adobe houses, wood-framed buildings, and early artifacts have been restored (see pp26–7).

5 Coronado

This idyllic community is famous for the Hotel del Coronado. Coronado's white sandy beaches, sidewalk cafés, and oceanfront mansions have enticed visitors for over a century (see pp28–9).

6 Point Loma
In 1542, Juan Cabrillo arrived at Ballast Point, claiming California for Spain. Now, stunning homes and marinas grace Point Loma's waterfront (see pp30–31).

7 Mission Basilica San Diego de Alcalá
Saint Junípero Serra established this mission in 1769 to Christianize the Native Americans (see pp32–3).

Around San Diego

Encinitas · Ramona · Julian
Green Mountains
Laguna Mtns
Lakeside · 79
El Cajon · 8 · 10 Mount Laguna
Pine Valley
Spring Valley · Live Oak Springs
San Ysidro · 94
Tijuana · MEXICO
Area of map below
0 km 20
0 miles 20

CLAIREMONT
SERRA MESA · GRANTVILLE
BAY PARK
LINDA VISTA · MISSION CITY · FRIARS RD
San Diego River · NORMAL HEIGHTS · 7
UNIVERSITY HEIGHTS · EL CAJON BLVD · FAIRMONT AVE
4 OLD TOWN · WASHINGTON ST · 8
NORTH PARK
PARK BLVD
DRIVE sland · PACIFIC HWY
3 GOLDEN HILL
2 · 1 DOWNTOWN BROADWAY
CORONADO · 94 · LOGAN HEIGHTS
5 ORANGE AVE · HARBOR DRIVE · 15
Spreckels Park · San Diego Bay
0 km 2
0 miles 2

8 Mission Bay Park
This aquatic wonderland epitomizes San Diego's laid-back life-style, from its watersports to the paths for cycling and strolling (see pp34–5).

9 La Jolla
This exclusive community is noted for the Scripps Institution of Oceanography, a world-renowned research facility (see pp36–7).

10 East County
About an hour east of the city, you can ride a vintage train, hike the forest, pan for gold, climb a mountain, and stargaze in the desert (see pp38–9).

🔟 ⭐ Gaslamp Quarter

Great nightclubs, trendy restaurants, and unique boutiques compete for attention in San Diego's most vibrant neighborhood. Alonzo Horton's 1867 New Town *(see p42)* seemed doomed to the wrecking ball in the 1970s, but a civic revitalization program transformed the dilapidated area into a showcase destination. By 1980, the Gaslamp Quarter was decreed a National Historic District.

1 Ingle Building
The Hard Rock Café was once known as the Golden Lion Tavern. Note the lion sculptures, stained-glass windows, and 1906 stained-glass dome over the bar.

NEED TO KNOW

MAP J5 ■ www.gaslamp.org

Ingle Building: 801 4th St

San Diego Hardware: 840 5th Ave

William Heath Davis House: 410 Island Ave (619) 233-4692; open 10am–5pm Tue–Sat, noon–4pm Sun; adm $10

Louis Bank of Commerce: 835 5th Ave

Keating Building: 432 F St

Lincoln Hotel: 536 5th Ave

Balboa Theatre: 868 4th Ave

Old City Hall: 664 5th Ave

Yuma Building: 643 5th Ave

■ Stop at the Ghirardelli Chocolate Shop (643 5th Ave) for a hot fudge sundae.

■ Parking is difficult on weekends. Take the San Diego Trolley; it stops right at Gaslamp.

■ Historical walking tours are held 1pm Thu (summer only), 5pm Fri & 11am Sat ($20; www.gaslampfoundation.org).

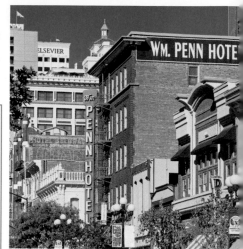

The historic buildings of the Gaslamp Quarter

2 San Diego Hardware
Once a dance hall, then a five-and-dime store, this building housed one of San Diego's oldest businesses, founded in 1892. Though the store relocated in 2006, the original storefront remains on Fifth Avenue.

3 William Heath Davis House
Named after the man who tried but failed to develop San Diego in 1850, the museum is home to the Gaslamp Quarter Historical Foundation. It's the oldest wooden structure in the downtown area.

4 Louis Bank of Commerce
A bank until 1893, this Victorian structure **(below)** was the favorite bar of Wyatt Earp *(see p43)*. It once contained the Golden Poppy Hotel, a notorious brothel.

6 Keating Building

Fannie Keating built this Romanesque-style building **(left)** in 1890 in honor of her husband George. It once housed some of the most prestigious offices in the whole town.

7 Lincoln Hotel

Built in 1913, the four-story tiled structure features Chinese elements, the original beveled glass in its upper stories, and its original green-and-white ceramic tile façade. Japanese prisoners were housed here before departing for internment camps during World War II.

STINGAREE DISTRICT

After its legitimate businesses relocated in the late 19th century, New Town was home to brothels, opium dens, saloons, and gambling halls, some operated by famous lawman Wyatt Earp. It became known as "Stingaree" because one could be stung on its streets as easily as by the stingaree fish in the bay. After police tried (and failed) to clean up Stingaree in 1912, it slowly disintegrated into a slum until rescued by the Gaslamp Quarter Foundation some 50 years later.

8 Balboa Theatre

This landmark 1,500-seat theater **(above)** started out as a grand cinema with waterfalls flanking the stage. Notice the beautiful tiled dome on the roof. A restoration project converted the building into a venue for live performances.

Gaslamp Quarter Map

5 Wrought-Iron Gas Lamps

San Diego's historic district is named after the quaint green wrought-iron gas lamps that line the streets– they actually run on electricity.

9 Old City Hall

Dating from 1874, this Italianate building features 16-ft (5-m) ceilings, brick arches, Classical columns, and a wrought-iron cage elevator. In 1900, the entire city government could fit inside. Today, the building houses condos, shops, and a restaurant.

10 Yuma Building

Captain Wilcox of the US *Invincible* owned downtown's first brick structure in 1888. The building was named for his business dealings in Yuma, Arizona. Airy residential lofts with large bay windows now occupy the upper levels of the building.

⭐ Embarcadero

Ever since Juan Cabrillo sailed into San Diego Bay in 1542 *(see p42)*, much of the city's life has revolved around its waterfront. Pioneers stepped ashore on its banks; immigrants worked as whalers and fishermen; the US Navy left an indelible mark with its shipyards and warships. Tourism has added another layer to the harbor's lively atmosphere. The Embarcadero welcomes visitors with its art displays, walkways, nautical museums, harbor cruises, and benches on which to sit and enjoy the uninterrupted harbor activity.

1 San Diego Harbor

One of the greatest attractions of the Embarcadero is the bustling harbor **(above)**, where you can watch as Navy destroyers, aircraft carriers, ferries, cruise ships, and sailboats glide past. Be a part of the action by taking a harbor cruise.

2 Seaport Village

New England and Spanish design blend eclectically in this waterfront area **(right)** with brilliant harbor views *(see p69)*.

3 San Diego County Administration Center

Dedicated by President F. Roosevelt, the 1936 civic structure looks especially magisterial at night. Enter through the west door and feel free to wander about *(see p48)*.

4 Tuna Harbor

San Diego was once home to the world's largest tuna fleet, with 200 commercial boats. Portuguese immigrants dominated the trade until the canneries moved to Mexico and Samoa. The US Tuna Foundation still keeps its offices here.

Map of the Embarcadero

7 San Diego Convention Center

The center **(above)** was designed to complement the waterfront location, with its flying buttresses, skylight tubes, and rooftop sails.

8 Piers

Glistening cruise ships bound for Mexico and the Panama Canal tie up at B Street Pier. Harbor cruises and ferries to Coronado can be caught nearby.

9 Santa Fe Depot

The train cars may be modern, but the atmosphere recalls the stylish days of rail travel. The interiors of the Spanish-Colonial style building **(right)** feature burnished oak benches, original tiles, and chandeliers.

10 Maritime Museum of San Diego

Nautical lovers can gaze at *Medea*, *San Salvador*, *Star of India*, *Berkeley*, and other vintage ships restored to their former glory *(see p47)*.

5 USS Midway Museum

The 1,000-ft (305-m) USS *Midway (see pp16–17)*, commissioned in 1945, was once the world's largest warship. Many docents on board are veterans of the carrier.

6 Embarcadero Marina Park

Relax on one of the grassy expanses to enjoy the excellent views of the harbor and Coronado Bridge. Joggers and bicyclists use the paths around the park *(see p51)*, and on weekends, entertainers and artists demonstrate their work.

NEED TO KNOW
MAP J6

Flagship Cruises: 990 N Harbor Dr; narrated tours: 1 hour $25; 2 hours $30; several departures daily *(see p114)*

USS Midway Museum: 910 N. Harbor Dr; (619) 544-9600; open 10am–5pm; adm adult $20, child $10

Santa Fe Depot: 1050 Kettner Blvd

■ For a quick bite, try Island Deli at 955 Harbor Island Drive. Their fresh sandwiches are good outdoor options.

■ Pedicabs are usually available to take you down to Seaport Village.

USS Midway Museum

1 Hangar Deck
The hangar deck stored the carrier's aircraft, with elevators raising planes up to the flight deck as needed. Now the carrier's entry level, it has audio-tour headsets, aircraft displays, a gift shop, café, and restrooms. Don't miss the 24-ft (7-m) Plexiglas model of the *Midway* used in World War II to construct the carrier.

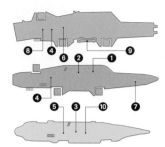

Key to Floor plan
- Roof Flight Deck and Island
- Hangar Deck and Forecastle
- 2nd, 3rd, and 4th Decks

Fighter plane on the hangar deck

2 Virtual Reality Flight Simulations
For an additional price, which also includes a briefing, a flight suit, and 30 minutes of flight, you can experience flying a plane by taking the controls of a flight simulator. Also on hand are several standard flight stations, where, for another ticket, you can practice taking off from a carrier.

3 Post Office
The *Midway*'s crew often had to wait several weeks at a time for a Carrier Onboard Delivery flight to receive letters from home. The post office was also in charge of the disbursement of money orders.

4 Aircraft
More than two dozen planes and helicopters are on display on the flight and hangar decks. Among the displays are the F-14A Tomcat, which flies at speeds exceeding Mach 2, two F-4 Phantoms, and an A-6E Intruder. The *Midway* once held up to 80 aircraft.

5 Galley
The *Midway* could store up to 1.5-million lbs (680,388 kg) of dry provisions and a quarter-million lbs (113,398 kg) of meat and vegetables to serve the crew 13,000 meals daily.

6 Flight Deck
The area of the *Midway*'s flight deck is roughly 4 acres (1.6 ha) in size. Additional aircraft are displayed here, and the Island is entered from here. The flight deck was where dramatic take-offs and landings took place – take-offs were from the bow, and the angled deck was used for landings.

Flight deck of the USS *Midway*

HISTORY OF THE MIDWAY

Commissioned on September 10, 1945, the *Midway* was named after the Battle of Midway, which was the turning point for the Allies in the War of the Pacific. She remained the largest ship in the world for ten years, and was the first ship too large to transit the Panama Canal. After the fall of Saigon on April 30, 1975, she saw further action during Operation Desert Storm in 1991, and finished her years of service by evacuating military personnel threatened by the 1991 eruption of Mount Pinatubo in the Philippines. The *Midway* was decommissioned in 1992.

TOP 10 MIDWAY STATISTICS

1 Overall length: 1,001 ft, 6 inches (305 m)

2 Width: 258 ft (78.6 m)

3 Height: 222 ft, 3 inches (67.7 m)

4 Full displacement: 70,000 tons (63,502,932 kg)

5 Number of propellers: 4

6 Weight of each propeller: 22 tons (19,958 kg)

7 Boilers: 12

8 Miles of piping: 200 (322 km)

9 Miles of copper conductor: 3,000 (4,828 km)

10 Ship fuel capacity: 2.23 million gallons (8.4 million liters)

Vietnam War anniversary gathering, USS *Midway*

7 Berths

Sleeping berths for 400 of the 4,500 crew members are displayed on the hangar deck. Beds were too short to be comfortable for anyone over 6 ft (1.8 m), and the accompanying metal lockers could hold barely more than a uniform. Enlisted men were often just out of high school.

8 Arresting Wire and Catapults

Notice the arresting wire on the flight deck. This enabled a pilot to land a 20-ton jet cruising at 150 miles (241 km) an hour on an area the size of a tennis court. A hook attached to the tail of a plane grabbed the wire during landing. Two steam catapults helped propel the plane for take-off.

9 Island

Ladders take you up to the navigation room and bridge, sometimes called the Superstructure, from where the ship's movements were commanded. The flight control deck oversaw aircraft operations.

The Island, or Superstructure

10 Metal Shop

On the mess deck, the metal shop produced metal structures and replicated metal parts for the ship or its aircraft. Self-sufficiency and versatility were the keywords for tours of duty when the ship would be away for months at a time.

TOP 10 ⭐ Balboa Park

Since the early 20th century, Balboa Park has awed San Diegans with its romantic hillside setting, lush landscaping, and splendid architecture. The park's magnificent Spanish structures date from the 1915–16 Panama-California Exposition. On weekends, thousands of visitors come to indulge their interests, whether it's recreational, Shakespeare, or art. However, the park is probably best known as the home of the world-famous San Diego Zoo, where almost 4,000 animals and 800 species reside.

Botanical Building ②

Constructed for the 1915–16 Panama-California Exposition, the Botanical Building **(right)** is one of the world's largest lath structures. It houses more than 2,100 orchids, palms, and other tropical plants, and seasonal flowers.

① Reuben H. Fleet Science Center

Explore sense and touch in the Gallery of Illusions and Perceptions **(above)**, learn about electricity, digital recording, and tornados, or catch an IMAX movie or a planetarium show *(see p59)*.

③ The Old Globe

The Tony-winning Old Globe Theatre, the Sheryl and Harvey White Theatre, and the Lowell Davies Festival Theatre form a wonderful cultural resource *(see p60)*.

BALBOA PARK AND WORLD WAR II

More than 2,000 beds were lined up in Balboa Park's museums for those wounded in 1941's Pearl Harbor attack. All buildings were used for barracks. The park became one of the largest hospital training centers in the world: 600 Navy nurses were stationed at the House of Hospitality, and the lily pond served as a rehab pool. In 1947, the military returned the park to the city.

④ Casa del Prado

This outstanding structure is a reconstruction of a building from the Panama-California Exposition. Wall reliefs commemorate Saint Junípero Serra and Juan Cabrillo.

⑤ Spanish Village Art Center

Architect Richard Requa *(see p43)* wanted visitors to experience the simple life of a Spanish village. This complex **(above)** houses 37 art and craft studios *(see p47)*.

6 **House of Hospitality**
Modeled on a hospital in Spain and now a visitor center, this was erected for the Panama-California Exposition and rebuilt in the 1990s.

7 **House of Pacific Relations**
Founded in 1935, these cottages feature cultural ambassadors from 33 countries showcasing local traditions.

Map of Balboa Park

10 **California Tower and Dome**
Built for the Exposition, this building (below), with its 200-ft (61-m) tower, has come to represent San Diego's identity. Famous figures of the city's past are represented on the façade. Inside is the Museum of Man (see p22).

8 **Spreckels Organ Pavilion**
One of the largest out-door organs in the world contains 4,530 pipes. The metal curtain protecting the organ weighs close to 12 tons. Free recitals are held on Sundays.

9 **San Diego Zoo**
In this zoo (see pp20–21), thousands of animals thrive in re-created natural habitats. Thanks to breeding programs and webcams, endangered baby pandas are now superstars.

San Diego Zoo

Giant pandas examining an enrichment toy in their enclosure

1 Panda Trek

The giant panda superstars spend most of their day eating bamboo, oblivious to the millions of adoring fans that line up for hours for a glimpse or to watch them via a 24-hour panda cam. Six panda births have occurred at the zoo in the last nine years, most recently male Xiao Liwu in July 2012. The area also features golden-hued takins, considered national treasures in China along with the pandas.

Scripps Aviary

2 Polar Bear Plunge

In this recreated Arctic tundra habitat, three huge polar bears lounge about and frolic in the chilly water of a 130,000-gallon plunge pool. Sometimes, for a special enrichment treat, zookeepers fill the enclosure with 18 tons of shaved snow for the bears to play in. Don't miss the pool viewing area down below; the bears often swim right up to the window.

3 Scripps Aviary

Inside a massive mesh cage, experience an exotic rainforest with sounds of cascading water and more than 130 screeching, chirping, and cawing African birds. Sit on a bench amid lush vegetation and try to spot a silvery-checked hornbill or gold-breasted starling.

4 Gorilla Tropics

These Western lowland gorillas romp and climb over wide areas of jungle and grassland. Parent gorillas lovingly tend to their children, while others sit quietly with chins in hand, contemplating the strange two-legged creatures observing them from the other side of the glass.

Map of San Diego Zoo

5 Lost Forest

Otis, several thousand pounds of male hippo, lives in a re-creation of the Congo River Basin with female Funani, who gave birth in 2015 to their daughter Devi. They share their jungle home with forest buffaloes, swamp monkeys, and okapis, whose long black prehensile tongues let them grab nearby leaves to eat.

6 Tiger River

A misty, orchid-filled rainforest is home to the endangered Malayan tiger. Marvel at these wondrous animals as they sit majestically on the rocks, waterfalls flowing behind them. This natural habitat was created to resemble their native jungle environment, with steep slopes, logs to climb on, and a warm cave near the viewing window.

Malayan tiger, Tiger River habitat

7 Reptile House

If it slithers, hisses, or rattles, it's here. Be glad these animals, especially the king cobra, Albino python, and Gila monsters, are behind glass. Cages marked with a red dot indicate the venomous ones.

8 Children's Zoo

Little ones love petting the goats and sheep in the paddock (wash-up sinks are nearby), while older kids squeal with mischievous glee at the tarantulas, black-widow spiders, and hissing cockroaches. The nursery takes care of baby animals whose mothers can't look after them.

An elephant in the Elephant Odyssey

9 Elephant Odyssey

The endangered elephants consume up to 125 lbs (57 kg) of hay and 30 gallons of water a day. Keep your camera ready, as the elephants often toss barrels or scratch their back under a special roller. Asian elephants have dome-shaped backs, while the ears of an African elephant are shaped like the African continent.

10 Conrad Prebys Australian Outback

Discover Australian wildlife from wombats to kookaburras – as many as seven different marsupials and 25 species of birds. The decks at the Queenslander House overlook a forest for the zoo's largest koala colony outside of Australia.

A koala at San Diego Zoo

Balboa Park Museums

1 San Diego Museum of Man

MAP L1 ■ (619) 239-2001
■ Open 10am–5pm daily ■ Adm
■ www.museumofman.org

Learn about evolution from a replica of a 4-million-year-old human ancestor, and visit the Ancient Egypt room for mummies and funerary objects. Artifacts from the Kumeyaay, San Diego's original inhabitants, and a replica of a Mayan monument emphasize the culture of the Americas.

2 San Diego Museum of Art

MAP L1 ■ (619) 232-7931 ■ Open 10am–5pm Mon, Tue & Thu–Sat; noon–5pm Sun ■ Adm ■ www. sdmart.org

This exceptional museum has works by old masters and major 19th- and 20th-century artists. Be sure to check out the Asian art collection.

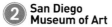
San Diego Museum of Art

3 Mingei International Museum

MAP L1 ■ (619) 239-0003
■ Open 10am–5pm Tue–Sun
■ Adm ■ www.mingei.org

The Japanese word *mingei* means "art of the people" and on view here is a display of international folk art. Exhibits include textiles, jewelry, furniture, and pottery.

San Diego Natural History Museum

4 San Diego Natural History Museum

MAP M1 ■ (619) 232-3821
■ Open 10am–5pm daily
■ Adm ■ www.sdnhm.org

Galleries showcase the evolution and diversity of California. Exhibits, guided weekend nature walks, and field trips explore the natural world.

5 Timken Museum of Art

MAP L1 ■ (619) 239-5548
■ Open 10am–4:30pm Tue–Sun (from noon Sun) ■ www.timkenmuseum.org

The collection includes Rembrandt's *Saint Bartholomew*, and works by Rubens and Bruegel the Elder.

6 San Diego History Center

MAP L1 ■ (619) 232-6203 ■ Open 10am–5pm daily ■ Adm ■ www. sandiegohistory.org

An alternating collection of old photographs and artifacts that introduce San Diego's early years.

7 Museum of Photographic Arts

MAP L1 ■ (619) 238-7559 ■ Open 10am–5pm Tue–Sun (to 8pm Thu in summer) ■ Adm ■ www.mopa.org

Temporary exhibitions featuring the world's most celebrated camera geniuses mix with pieces from the museum's permanent collection. The theater screens film classics.

8 San Diego Air and Space Museum

MAP L2 ■ (619) 234-8291
■ Open 10am–4:30pm daily ■ Adm
■ www.sandiegoairandspace.org

One of the museum's finest planes, the Lockheed A-12 Blackbird spy plane, greets you on arrival. Don't miss the International Aerospace Hall of Fame.

Map of the Balboa Park Museums

9 San Diego Automotive Museum

MAP L2 ■ (619) 231-2886 ■ Open 10am–5pm daily ■ Adm ■ www.sdautomuseum.org

Discover California's car culture through classic vehicles and rotating and permanent exhibits. A Racing Hall of Fame honors past giants of the racing world.

San Diego Automotive Museum

10 San Diego Hall of Champions Sports Museum

MAP L2 ■ (619) 234-2544
■ Open 10am–4:30pm daily ■ Adm ■ www.sdhoc.com

Items celebrating San Diego's sports heroes are exhibited here. Inspiring displays cover more than 40 different sports.

THE MOTHER OF BALBOA PARK

Horticulturalist Kate Sessions needed room to establish a nursery in 1910. She struck a deal with the city of San Diego in which she promised to plant 100 trees a year in the then-called City Park and 300 trees elsewhere in exchange for 36 acres. A 35-year planting frenzy resulted in 10,000 glorious trees and shrubs, shady arbors draped with bougainvillea, and flower gardens that burst with color throughout the year.

**TOP 10
GARDENS OF
BALBOA PARK**

1 Alcázar Gardens

2 Japanese Friendship Garden

3 Botanical Building and Lily Ponds

4 Palm Canyon

5 Casa del Rey Moro

6 Zoro Garden

7 Rose Garden

8 Desert Garden

9 Florida Canyon

10 Moreton Bay Fig Tree

The Alcázar Gardens look particularly beautiful and colorful when in full bloom during the spring.

Following pages Desert sand verbena and desert primrose, Anza-Borrego Desert State Park

TOP10 ⭐ Old Town State Historic Park

After Mexico won its independence from Spain in 1821, many retired soldiers created what is now Old Town, laying their homes and businesses around the plaza in typical Spanish style. Through trade with Boston, the town began to prosper. After a fire in 1872 destroyed much of the commercial center, San Diego moved to a "New Town" closer to the bay. Today, you can explore the preserved and restored structures of San Diego's pioneer families.

1 Plaza

Spanish communities used the plaza for bullfights, political events, executions, and fiestas. Since 1846, tradition maintains that the Old Town flagpole must be made from a ship's mast.

La Casa de Estudillo 2

Built in 1827 by José Estudillo, the Presidio's commander, this adobe home (right) is Old Town's showpiece. Workmen shaped the curved red tiles of the roof by spreading clay over their legs.

3 Seeley Stable Museum

Before railroads, Albert Seeley ran a stagecoach business between San Diego and LA. This barn houses original carriages and wagons from the Wild West (below).

4 Mason Street School

This one-room school opened in 1865. Its first teacher, Mary Chase Walker, resigned her $65-a-month position when townspeople complained that she had invited a black woman to lunch.

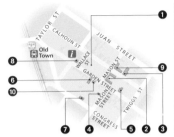

Map of Old Town State Historic Park

FIRST IMPRESSIONS

In his epic story of early San Diego, *Two Years Before the Mast* (1840), Richard Henry Dana described the town as "a small settlement directly before the fort, composed of about 40 dark-brown-looking huts or houses, and two larger ones plastered." Bostonian Mary Chase Walker, San Diego's first schoolhouse teacher, was more blunt: "Of all the dilapidated, miserable looking places I had ever seen, this was the worst."

5 San Diego Union Historical Museum

This wood-frame house was built in New England and shipped down in 1851. It was home to the early years of *The San Diego Union*, the city's oldest newspaper.

7 La Casa de Machado y Stewart

Jack Stewart married Rosa Machado in 1845 and moved to this adobe home, where the family remained until 1966. Its deterioration finally forced them to move.

8 Robinson-Rose House

Docents are on hand to answer questions at this house, which dates from 1853 and is the head-quarters of Old Town. Look out for the model of the 1872 Old Town.

9 La Casa de Bandini

Peruvian Juan Bandini arrived in San Diego in 1819 and became one of its wealthiest citizens. His former home is now the Cosmopolitan Hotel (below).

6 Colorado House

The name Wells Fargo came to symbolize the opening of the American West. At this little museum housed in a former hotel (above), a restored stagecoach is the main exhibit.

NEED TO KNOW

MAP N5 ▪ 4002 Wallace St ▪ (619) 220-5422 ▪ www.parks.ca.gov

Open May–Sep 10am–5pm daily; Oct–Apr 10am–4pm Mon–Thu, 10am–5pm Fri & Sat

La Casa de Estudillo: closed Mon

Seeley Stable Museum: closed Tue

▪ Head to one of San Diego's most famous Mexican restaurants, Old Town Mexican Café & Cantina (see p89), and watch the ladies make tortillas as you have lunch.

▪ One-hour walking tours led by park staff leave daily at 11am and 2pm from the Robinson-Rose House.

▪ Park concessionaires sell traditional souvenirs and other wares; nearby Bazaar del Mundo offers colorful, unique items.

10 First San Diego Courthouse

This reconstruction of the 1847 courthouse marks the city's first fire-brick structure. Not to be missed is the ominous 1860 jail cell out back.

🔟⭐ Coronado

Sometimes described as an island because its village-like atmosphere is far removed from the big city, picturesque Coronado lies on a sliver of land between the Pacific Ocean and San Diego Bay. More retired Navy officers live here than any other place in the US, and although the military presence is high, it's unobtrusive. For over 100 years, visitors have flocked to Coronado to be part of this charmed life. Even with its thriving resorts, restaurants, sidewalk cafés, and unique shops, the village never seems overwhelmed.

Hotel del Coronado ①
This 1887–8 Queen Anne wooden masterpiece **(right)** is a National Historic Landmark. It was the first hotel west of the Mississippi with electric lights.

② Meade House
L. Frank Baum moved to Coronado in 1904 and produced much of his work at this charming house, now a private residence.

③ US Naval Amphibious Base
South of Coronado, along the Silver Strand, this training camp for the hallowed Navy SEALS is off-limits to the public.

NEED TO KNOW

MAP C6 ■ www.coronadovisitorcenter.com

Hotel del Coronado: 1500 Orange Ave; (619) 435-6611; www.hoteldel.com

Meade House: 1101 Star Park Cir

Ferry Landing Market Place: 1201 1st St at B Ave; (619) 435-8895; open 10am daily, various closing times

Coronado Museum of History and Art: 1100 Orange Ave; (619) 435-7242; open 9am–5pm Mon–Fri, 10am–5pm Sat & Sun; adm $5; www.coronadohistory.org

Coronado to San Diego Ferry: (619) 234-4111; adm $4.25

■ Enjoy the Hotel del Coronado's ambience by having a drink in the Babcock & Story Bar.

■ Excellent historical walking tours depart from Glorietta Bay Inn, 1630 Glorietta Blvd; (619) 435-5993; Tue, Thu & Sat at 11am; adm.

④ Coronado Bridge
Connecting San Diego to Coronado since 1969, this 2.2-mile (3.5-km) span **(above)** has won architectural awards for its unique design. Struts and braces in a box girder give it a sleek look.

⑤ Coronado Central Beach
Coronado's main beach claims a golden swath adjacent to the Hotel del Coronado. Families, fishers, surfers, and swimmers all stake spots, while dog-walkers rule the north end.

6 Mansions along Ocean Boulevard

Designed by prominent early 20th-century architects Hebbard and Gill, mansions **(above)** dominate Coronado's oceanfront.

Map of Coronado

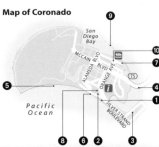

7 Ferry Landing Marketplace

Next to the ferry dock is a shopping area selling beachwear, jewelry, and souvenirs, and art. This is a handy spot to rent a bike or grab a snack.

8 Coronado Museum of History and Art

In a 1910 Neo-Classical bank building, galleries exhibit early village history, with photos of the Hotel del Coronado, Tent City, and military memorabilia **(right)**.

9 San Diego Ferry

Before the Coronado Bridge, access was only by a long drive around Southern San Diego or via the ferry, which is now only for foot passengers.

10 Orange Avenue

The main shopping street has restaurants and sidewalk cafés, as well as a theater and a museum. Independence Day and Christmas parades see residents out celebrating.

THE DUKE AND DUCHESS OF WINDSOR

When the British King Edward VIII gave up his throne to marry American Wallis Simpson, romantics insisted they originally met at the Hotel del Coronado. In 1920, Wallis Spencer, then married to a naval officer of that name, lived at the hotel. That April, Edward visited Coronado. It is unclear whether the couple met then; it wasn't until 15 years later that they were formally introduced.

TOP 10 ⭐ Point Loma

Point Loma was once one of the roughest areas in San Diego. The city's first boats were tied up here, followed by the largest whaling operation on the West Coast and leather tanning and tallow production. Today, sailboats and lavish yachts grace the marinas of Point Loma, and the waterfront homes make up some of the most expensive real estate in the city. The Cabrillo National Monument, one of the most visited monuments in the US, boasts the most breathtaking views of the entire city.

1 Cabrillo National Monument

The spot where Cabrillo stepped ashore is on a spit of land downhill at Ballast Point. This statue (below) is a worthy tribute to the brave explorer and his men who traversed the seas to claim new territory for Spain.

Yachts anchored at the marinas at Point Loma

2 Old Point Loma Lighthouse

This Cape Cod-style building was completed in 1855. Unfortunately, coastal fog often hid the beacon light, so another lighthouse, the New Point Loma Lighthouse, was built below the cliff.

3 Tide Pools

Now protected by law, starfish, anemones, warty sea cucumbers and wooly sculpins thrive in their own little world.

4 Bayside Trail

A 2-mile (3.2-km) round-trip hiking path runs on an old military defense road. Signs on the way identify over 300 indigenous plants such as sage scrub and Indian paintbrush.

5 Sunset Cliffs

A path runs along the edge of these spectacular 400-ft (122-m) high cliffs (below), but signs emphatically warn of their instability. Access the beach from Sunset Cliffs Park.

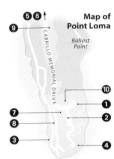

Map of Point Loma

Ballast Point

CABRILLO MEMORIAL DRIVE

7 Military Exhibit

After the 1941 Pearl Harbor attack, many felt that San Diego would be the next target. The exhibit explores how the military created a coastal defense system and the largest gun in the US.

8 Whale Overlook

Pacific gray whales migrate yearly to give birth in the warm, sheltered waters of Baja California before heading back to Alaska for a summer of good eating. January and February are the best times to spot whales.

JUAN CABRILLO

After participating in the conquest of Mexico and Guatemala, Juan Cabrillo was instructed to explore the northern limits of the West Coast of New Spain in search of gold and a route to Asia. He arrived at Ballast Point on September 28, 1542, claimed the land for Spain, and named it San Miguel. Cabrillo died a few months later from complications of a broken bone. Spain saw the expedition as a failure and left the territory untouched for more than 200 years.

9 Fort Rosecrans National Cemetery

The southern end of Point Loma belongs to the military installations of Rosecrans Fort. Innumerable crosses mark the graves **(above)** of more than 100,000 US veterans, some of whom died at the Battle of San Pasqual in the Mexican-American War.

6 Point Loma Nazarene University

Once a yoga commune, much of the original architecture of this Christian university is still intact.

10 Visitor Center

Browse through the center's outstanding books about the Spanish, Native Americans, and early California, or enjoy the daily film screenings. Park rangers are on hand to answer questions.

NEED TO KNOW
MAP B6

Cabrillo National Monument Visitor Center: 1800 Cabrillo Memorial Drive; (619) 557-5450; open 9am–5pm daily; adm $10 per vehicle; $5 per person (cyclists and walk-ins); tickets last for 7 days and visitors can return as many times as they like; www.nps.gov/cabr

■ Vending machines at the Cabrillo National Monument Visitor Center offer snacks. If you want to spend the day exploring the tide pools or hiking, bring food and water.

■ Bring binoculars to enjoy the views and, if visiting the tide pools, shoes with plenty of grip.

■ The San Diego Metropolitan Transit comes out to the monument. Take bus 28 or 84c from the Old Town Transportation Center.

TOP 10 ★ Mission Basilica San Diego de Alcalá

Founded by Saint Junípero Serra in 1769, this was California's first mission. Serra encouraged Native Americans to live here, exchanging work in the fields for religious instruction. Harassment by soldiers and lack of water supplies caused the mission to be moved from its original location in Old Town to this site. In 1976, Pope Paul VI bestowed the mission with the status of minor basilica. In 2015, Pope Francis canonized Junípero Serra, the first such ceremony to be conducted on US soil.

1 La Casa del Padre Serra

The original 1774 adobe walls and beams **(below)** survived a Native American attack, military occupation, earthquakes, and years of neglect. Padres lived simply, with few material comforts.

2 Campanario

This graceful 46-ft (14-m) bell tower **(right)** defines California mission architecture. One of the bells is considered an original, and the crown atop another suggests it was probably cast in a royal foundry.

3 Padre Luis Jayme Museum

Artifacts here include records of births and deaths in Saint Serra's handwriting, the last crucifix he held, and old photographs showing the extent of the mission's dereliction prior to restoration efforts.

4 Garden Statues

Four charming statues of St. Anthony of Padua **(right)**, patron saint of the Native Americans; St. Serra; St. Joseph, saint of Serra's expedition; and St. Francis keep vigil over the inner garden.

5 Chapel

Taken from a Carmelite monastery in Plasencia, Spain, this small chapel features choir stalls, a throne, and an altar dating from the 1300s. The choir stalls are held together by grooves rather than nails. The raised seats allowed the monks to stand while singing.

JUNÍPERO SERRA

Franciscan father Saint Junípero Serra spent 20 years in Mexico before coming to California. Few of his companions survived the tough "Sacred Expedition" across the desert. Serra, undeterred, established California's first mission in 1769. His sainthood was controversial for many Native Americans as they felt the mission system had helped to fragment their culture.

8 Church

The width of a mission church depended on available beams. Restored to specifications of a former 1813 church on this site, the church **(left)** features adobe bricks, the original floor tiles, and wooden door beams.

9 Padre Luis Jayme Memorial

On November 5, 1775, Native Americans attacked the mission. A cross marks the approximate spot where the Kumeyaay tribe killed Jayme, California's first martyr.

Mission Basilica San Diego de Alcalá

NEED TO KNOW

MAP E3 ■ 10818 San Diego Mission Road ■ (619) 281-8449 ■ www.mission sandiego.com

Open 9am–4:45pm daily ■ Adm $3, Tote-a-Tape Tours $2

Church: Mass 7am & 5:30pm Mon–Fri, 5:30pm Sat, 7am, 8am, 9am, 10am, 11am, noon & 5:30pm Sun

■ Food and drinks are not allowed inside the mission.

■ Be aware that the San Diego Trolley stops a good three blocks away.

6 Cemetery

Although it no longer contains real graves, this is the oldest cemetery in California. The crosses are made of original mission tiles. A memorial honors Native Americans who died during the mission era.

7 El Camino Real

Also called the Royal Road or King's Highway, this linked the state's 21 missions, each a day's distance apart on foot.

10 Gardens

Exotic plants add to the lush landscape around the mission **(above)**. With few indigenous Californian plants available, missionaries and settlers brought plants from all parts of the world, including cacti from Mexico and bird of paradise from South Africa.

TOP 10 ⭐ Mission Bay Park

In 1542, explorer Juan Rodriguez Cabrillo named this tidal basin "False Bay." Between the 1940s and 1960s, the US Army Corps of Engineers transformed the swampland into a 6.5-sq-mile (17-sq-km) showplace aquatic park and the city's premier recreational playground. Containing 19 miles (30 km) of beach and 27 miles (43 km) of shoreline, Mission Bay offers water and land sports, as well as cozy inlets and grassy knolls for lazy days.

4 DeAnza Cove
On the northeast corner of the park, DeAnza is convenient for a picnic or swim. Boats and jet skis launch from the ramp, and there is a designated area for volleyball.

6 Ventura Bridge
Extending 116 ft (35 m) across Mission Bay Drive, Ventura Bridge connects Quivira and Mariners basins, before linking to Mission Beach and Belmont Park.

1 Fiesta Island
Reached via a causeway, this dune-covered peninsular park **(above)** has bonfire rings and a leash-free dog area. The site also hosts the infamous Over the Line tournament.

2 Mission Bay Aquatic Center
Known as one of the world's largest facilities of its kind, this center at Santa Clara Point offers lessons in nearly every water activity, from surfing and sailing to paddleboard yoga and sea kayaking.

3 Bayside Walk
Strollers or cyclists may take this route from the lush Catamaran Resort (the departure point for sternwheeler Bahia Belle) to the park's western edge, where it loops at Mission Point. Rest and take in the views along the path.

5 Mariners Point
Jutting from the tip of a small peninsula, this sandy expanse provides an intriguing dichotomy: it hosts skateboard competitions and is a nesting site for the California least tern **(below)**.

7 Mission Beach and Ocean Front Walk
Parallel to Mission Beach, Ocean Front Walk is more of a movement than a stroll, a chaotic blend of rollerbladers, skate dancers, cyclists, and surfers running toward the waves. Festivities continue onto Mission Beach – a gigantic 2-mile (3-km), year-round beach party.

8 Belmont Park

Belmont Park **(below)** still retains its old-fashioned seaside aura, highlighted by the 1925 Giant Dipper roller coaster, but there are also attractions like *Tron*-themed laser tag and the FlowBarrel artificial wave machine *(see p59)*.

9 Crystal Pier

The dividing line between Pacific and Mission beaches, this 750-ft (228-m) pier **(above)** is notable for its 1930s cottage motel, set right above the water. Even if you don't book a stay at the motel, you can still walk the pier.

10 Quivira Basin

Waterfront shops, restaurants, and a resort are clustered around busy Quivira Basin and Dana Landing, from where daily scuba diving and fishing charters depart. Mission Bay Park Headquarters provides information and maps. From Dana Landing, Ingraham Street cuts across Vacation Isle to Crown Point.

Map of Mission Bay Park

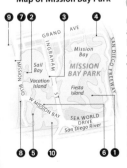

NEED TO KNOW

MAP B4

Mission Bay Park Headquarters: 2581 Quivira Court, San Diego 92109; (619) 221-8899, recorded info (619) 221-8824; www.sandiego.gov/lifeguards/about/contact

Mission Bay Aquatic Center: 1001 Santa Clara Place, San Diego 92109; (858) 488-1000; **Open** 8am–7pm daily. Equipment for hire such as sailboats, kayaks, bodyboards, paddleboards, and more (terms and conditions apply). Lessons and classes: rates vary (www.mbaquatic center.com).

Bahia Belle: 998 West Mission Bay, San Diego 92109; (858) 539-7779 for tickets and public cruises. Boarding times: Bahia Hotel, 6:30pm–1:30am; Catamaran Resort, 7pm–1am; adm $10, under 12s $3 (free for resort guests). Minors must be accompanied by a parent or guardian; minimum age for boarding after family hour (6:30–9pm) is 21 with valid ID. www.bahiahotel.com/dining-entertainment/bahia-belle-boat-cruise

Belmont Park: 3146 Mission Blvd, San Diego 92109; (858) 228-9283; rides open 11am–10pm most days. Free parking and admission; ride prices vary

TOP 10 ⭐ La Jolla

Developer Frank Botsford bought a substantial area of barren pueblo land in 1886, which he then subdivided. Other real estate developers soon caught on to La Jolla's potential and built resorts, but it wasn't until Ellen Browning Scripps arrived in 1896 that the town developed as a research, education, and art center. Now, La Jolla (pronounced "hoya") is among the most expensive land in the US. Befittingly, its name translates as "the jewel."

1 La Jolla Bay
This gathering spot **(above)** just below La Jolla village is small but startling, wedged between sandstone cliffs with glorious views. Its robust marine life is protected.

3 Museum of Contemporary Art
Only a fraction of more than 3,000 works from every noteworthy art movement since 1950 are on display at this renowned museum.

2 La Jolla Playhouse
The Tony Award-winning Playhouse **(below)**, founded by actor Gregory Peck, resides in the UC San Diego Theatre district *(see p60)*.

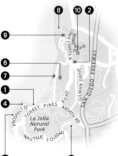

Map of La Jolla

4 Ellen Browning Scripps Park
Stroll along palm-lined walkways and gaze out over panoramic coastline views.

6 Birch Aquarium at Scripps

Brilliantly colored underwater habitats educate at this marine museum **(left)**. You'll feel like a scuba diver when viewing sharks swimming in an offshore kelp bed housed in a 70,000-gallon tank *(see p59)*.

7 Scripps Institution of Oceanography

Leading the way in global science research, Scripps Oceanography is now in its second century of discovery. Hundreds of research programs are under way on every continent and ocean.

8 Torrey Pines State Reserve

At this reserve *(see p50)*, hiking trails wind past coastal scrub, sandstone cliffs, and woodlands, with stunning views of the Pacific. Guided tours are available.

5 Mount Soledad Veterans Memorial

The 43-ft (13-m) cross on Mount Soledad, erected in 1954, is the centerpiece of a memorial that honors veterans of the Korean and other wars. Six walls beneath the cross hold 2,400 plaques.

ELLEN BROWNING SCRIPPS

Born in England in 1836, Scripps moved to the US in 1844. She became a teacher, investing her savings in her brother's newspaper ventures in Detroit and Cleveland. Already wealthy, she inherited a fortune on his death in 1900. Scripps spent her last 35 years in La Jolla, giving away millions of dollars for the good of humanity.

9 Salk Institute

Dr. Jonas Salk, creator of the first successful polio vaccine, founded this institution for biomedical research in 1960 *(see p48)*.

10 University of California, San Diego (UCSD)

Six colleges make up one of the most prestigious public universities **(below)** in the country.

NEED TO KNOW

MAP A2

Museum of Contemporary Art: 700 Prospect St; (858) 454-3541; open 11am–5pm Thu–Tue; 11am–7pm 3rd Thu each month; adm $10; free 5–7pm third Thu of month; www.mcasd.org

Mount Soledad: Soledad Rd; open 7am–10pm daily

Scripps Institution of Oceanography: 8622 Kennel Way; www.sio.ucsd.edu

University of California, San Diego: 9500 Gilman Dr; (858) 534-2230; www.ucsd.edu

■ The café at the Museum of Contemporary Art serves good sandwiches and salads.

■ Watch the paragliders launch from the Torrey Pines cliffs, or stroll the UCSD campus and its Stuart Collection of outdoor sculpture.

TOP 10 ⭐ East County

San Diego's East County offers truly diverse attractions within an hour or so of downtown. Interstate 8 passes Indian casinos and the vintage trains at Campo, with a turnoff to Cuyamaca Rancho State Park. Scenic backroad State Route 78 hits the gold-rush mountain village of Julian. Both roads take in Anza-Borrego Desert State Park.

1 Cuyamaca Rancho State Park

Just 5 miles (8 km) north of I-8, Cuyamaca **(below)** has more than 100 miles (160 km) of hiking, biking, and horse trails, with desert and coast views along the way. A creek meanders through Green Valley.

2 Indian Casinos

San Diego's Indian tribes have more than a dozen 24-hour casinos in the county, with slots, table games, bingo, and off-track betting, as well as entertainment. Only those over 21 and with valid identification are allowed in gaming areas.

3 Julian

After the gold rush of the 1870s, some stayed on in this charming community **(below)** surrounded by forests in the Cuyamaca Mountains. Filled with B&Bs, this Historical District is a popular weekend getaway and known for its apple orchards.

4 Desert Blooms

On first glimpse, this desert may look like a gigantic expanse of nothingness, but it is rife with life, notably wildflowers and bird species. Between February and April, weather permitting, it erupts into a vibrant palette of colorful blooms **(below)**.

5 Driving Tours

Venturing into the desert by car, other than on the main roads, is not advisable for the inexperienced. Roads can be impassable and unpredictable. A variety of tour operators can safely escort you on everything from a short day tour to an off-road overnight adventure.

(8) Borrego Springs

San Diego County's desert community **(left)** has lodging, restaurants, tours, and the Park Headquarters, where you can view exhibits, an informative film, and a desert garden.

METAL DINOSAURS

Mexico native and California resident, sculptor Ricardo Breceda made the metal "dinosaurs" that pop out of the desert-scape. Breceda created more than 130 full-sized replicas of creatures that once roamed these lands, including desert tortoises, saber-toothed cats, wild horses, and a 350-ft (106-m) serpent.

(6) Pacific Southwest Railway

Operated by the Railway Museum of San Diego, the *Golden State Limited* departs twice daily on weekends from the historic Campo train depot for a 12-mile (20-km) round trip to Miller Creek.

(9) Anza-Borrego Desert State Park

California's largest state park (938 sq miles/ 2,430 sq km) offers cacti and posies, rough trails, historic roads, mountainous dunes, extreme temperatures, other-worldly skies – plus peace and quiet.

Map of East County

(10) Tecate (Mexico)

This Mexican border town is about 20 minutes west via State Route 94. Check with the US Border Patrol for any up-to-the-minute safety issues, as well as any needed re-entry visa. If possible, simply park your car in the little lot by the border (someone will come out to take a few dollars) and walk across.

(7) Mount Laguna

After a good storm, this 5,738-ft- (1,750-m-) high hamlet at the eastern edge of the Cleveland National Forest becomes a winter playground for San Diegans, who come here to sled, cross-country ski, and generally marvel at the chillier climes.

NEED TO KNOW
MAP F2

Anza-Borrego Desert State Park Visitor Center: 200 Palm Canyon Dr, Borrego Springs ▪ (760) 767-5311

Open Year-round; visitor center open 9am–5pm Oct–May plus weekends & hols Jun–Sep ▪ Adm $8 per vehicle at Borrego Palm Canyon Campground in season, $6 other months.

Camping reservations (can be made up to 7 months in advance): (800) 444-7275

Borrego Springs Chamber of Commerce: 786 Palm Canyon Dr; Borrego Springs; (760) 767-5555; www.borregosprings chamber.com

This is a good source for reputable tour operators for off-road excursions and stargazing treks.

▪ If crossing the border into Mexico, assure your personal safety and that of your property. Heed US State Department warnings: www.state. gov/travel

The Top 10 of Everything

**A stage show at the
La Jolla Playhouse**

🔟 Moments in History

1 In the Beginning

A skull discovered in 1929 established human presence in San Diego about 12,000 years ago. The Kumeyaay tribe, present at the time of Cabrillo's landing, lived in small, organized villages, and subsisted on acorns, berries, and small prey.

2 Discovery by Juan Cabrillo (1542)

Cabrillo (see p31) was the first European to land at San Diego Bay. The Spanish believed that Baja and Alta California were part of a larger island, "Isla California," named for a legendary land in a Spanish 15th-century romance. California was part of the Spanish Empire for the next 279 years.

Juan Cabrillo

3 The Spanish Settlement (1769)

Fearing the loss of California, Spain sent an expedition, led by Gaspar de Portolá and Franciscan friar Junípero Serra (see p32), to build military posts and Christian missions. Disastrous for the Native Americans, the settlement survived and a city slowly took hold.

The Spanish Settlement

4 Mexico Gains Independence (1821)

After gaining independence, Mexico secularized the California missions and gave their land to the politically faithful. The rancho system of land management lasted into the 1900s. Ports were open to all and San Diego became a center for the hide trade.

5 California Becomes a State (1850)

The Mexican era lasted only until 1848. One bloody battle between the Americans and Californios was fought at San Pasqual (see p45). With a payment of $15 million and the treaty of Guadalupe Hidalgo, California became part of the US and, later, its 31st state.

6 Alonzo Horton Establishes a New City (1867)

Horton realized an investment opportunity to develop a city closer to the water than Old Town. He bought 960 acres for $265, then sold and gave lots to anyone who could build a brick house. Property values soared, especially after a fire in 1872 in Old Town. "New Town" became today's San Diego.

7 Transcontinental Railroad Arrives (1885)

Interest was renewed in San Diego when the Transcontinental Railroad reached town. Real estate speculators poured in, infrastructure was built, and the future looked bright. However, Los Angeles seemed more promising, and San Diego's population, having gone from 5,000 to 40,000 in two years, shrank to 16,000.

8 Panama-California Exposition (1915–16)

To celebrate the opening of the Panama Canal and draw economic attention to the first US port of call on the West Coast, Balboa Park *(see pp18–19)* was made into an attraction. Fair animals found homes at the zoo *(see pp20–21)* and Spanish-Colonial buildings became park landmarks.

California-Pacific Exposition

9 California-Pacific Exposition (1935–6)

A new Balboa Park exposition was launched to help alleviate effects of the Great Depression. The architect Richard Requa designed buildings inspired by Aztec, Mayan, and Pueblo Indian themes.

10 World War II

The founding of the aircraft industry, spurred by the presence of Ryan Aviation and Convair, gave San Diego an enduring industrial base. After Pearl Harbor, the Pacific Fleet HQ moved here. The harbor was enlarged, and hospitals, camps, and housing changed the city's landscape.

TOP 10 FAMOUS SAN DIEGO FIGURES

The author Theodore Geisel

1 Father Luis Jayme (1740–75)
California's first Christian martyr died in a Native American attack *(see p33)*.

2 Richard Henry Dana (1815–82)
Author of the 19th-century classic *Two Years Before the Mast*, a historical record of early San Diego *(see p27)*.

3 William Heath Davis (1822–1909)
This financier *(see p12)* established a new settlement known as "Davis' Folly."

4 Alonzo Horton (1813–1909)
Real estate magnate Horton, the "father" of San Diego, successfully established the city's present location in 1867.

5 Wyatt Earp (1848–1929)
Old West sheriff and famed gunman Earp owned saloons and gambling halls in the Gaslamp Quarter *(see p12)*.

6 John D. Spreckels (1853–1926)
Spreckels, a generous philanthropist and businessman, was the owner of the Hotel del Coronado.

7 L. Frank Baum (1856–1919)
The author of the *Wonderful Wizard of Oz* lived in and considered Coronado an "earthly paradise" *(see p28)*.

8 Charles Lindbergh (1902–74)
Lindbergh was the first to fly solo across the Atlantic in 1927.

9 Theodore Geisel (1904–91)
Best known as the beloved Dr. Seuss, Geisel lived and worked in La Jolla.

10 Dr. Jonas Salk (1914–95)
Developed the first effective polio vaccination, licensed for use in 1955, and founded the non-profit Salk Institute *(see p48)* in 1960.

🔟 Historic Sites

1 Ballast Point
MAP B6 ▪ Point Loma

In 1542, while the Kumeyaay tribe waited on a beach at Ballast Point, Juan Cabrillo (see p31) stepped ashore and claimed the land for Spain. In 1803, the "Battle of San Diego Bay" took place here, after Spanish Fort Guijarros fired on an American brig in a smuggling incident.

Entrance to a courtyard in Old Town

2 Old Town

After Mexico won its independence from Spain in 1821, retired soldiers and their families moved downhill from the presidio, built homes, and opened businesses. An open trade policy attracted others to settle, and by the end of the decade, 600 people lived in Old Town – San Diego's commercial and residential center until 1872.

3 Presidio Hill
MAP P5

Spain established its presence in California atop this hill, and Saint Serra founded the first California mission (see pp32–3) here. During the Mexican-American War in 1846, Fort Stockton, made of earthworks on top of the hill, changed hands thrice between Mexican-Californian ranchers, known as Californios.

4 Lindbergh Field
MAP C5

San Diego International Airport (see p93) was popularly called Lindbergh Field after Charles Lindbergh (see p43), who began the first leg of his transatlantic crossing here in 1927. The US Army Air Corps drained the surrounding marshland, took over the small airport, and enlarged the runways to accommodate the heavy bomber aircraft manufactured in San Diego during World War II.

5 Julian
MAP F2

The discovery of gold in the hills northeast of San Diego in 1870 was the largest strike in Southern California. For five years, miners poured into the town of Julian (see p38), which would have become the new county seat if San Diego supporters had not plied the voters of Julian with liquor on election day. The gold eventually ran out, but not until millions of dollars were pumped into San Diego's economy.

6 Mission Basilica San Diego de Alcalá

Originally built on Presidio Hill in 1769, this mission moved up the valley a few years later. It was the first of 21 missions as well as the birthplace of Christianity in California. It was the only mission to be attacked by Indians. In 1847, the US Cavalry occupied the grounds (see pp32–3).

Mission Basilica San Diego de Alcalá

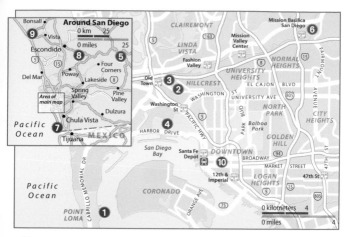

7 Border Field State Park
MAP E3 ∎ (619) 575-3613
∎ Call for opening hours

The Mexican-American War ended with the signing of the Treaty of Guadalupe Hidalgo (see p42) on February 2, 1848. A US and Mexican Boundary Commission then determined the new international border between the two countries, with California divided into Alta and Baja. A marker placed in 1851 on a bluff in this park shows the farthest western point of the new border.

8 San Pasqual Battlefield State Historic Park
MAP E2 ∎ 15808 San Pasqual Valley Rd, Escondido ∎ Open 8am–5pm Sat & Sun

On December 6, 1846, a volunteer army of Californios, defeated the invading American army in one of the bloodiest battles of the Mexican-American War. Though the Californios won the battle, they later lost the war, and California became part of the US.

9 Mission San Luis Rey de Francia

Nicknamed the "King of Missions" for its size, wealth, and vast agricultural estates, this mission is the largest adobe structure in California. The Franciscan padres Christianized 3,000 Indians here. After secularization, the mission fell into disrepair and was used for a time as military barracks. It has since been restored to its former glory (see p99).

10 Gaslamp Quarter

Filled with late-19th-century Victorian architecture, this historic site was once the commercial heart of Alonzo Horton's (see p42) New Town. When development moved north to Broadway, the area filled with gambling halls and brothels. It was revitalized in the 1970s (see pp12–13).

Gaslamp Quarter

🔟 Museums and Art Galleries

San Diego Museum of Art, Balboa Park

1 Museums of Balboa Park

Housed in stunning structures of Spanish-Colonial, Mayan, and Aztec designs, exhibits at these acclaimed museums constantly change, making Balboa Park (see pp18–19) a year-round attraction. Enjoy fine art, photography, aerospace, anthropology, model trains, and much more (see pp22–3).

2 Museum of Contemporary Art

The most important contemporary art trends are presented at this museum. Docent-led tours, lectures, and special family nights make art accessible to all. The museum's flagship facility (see p36) is at the former oceanfront home of Ellen Browning Scripps (see p37), with a satellite location downtown (see p79).

3 San Diego Chinese Historical Museum

MAP J5 ■ 404 3rd Ave ■ (619) 338-9888 ■ Open 10:30am–4pm Tue–Sat, noon–4pm Sun ■ Adm ■ www.sdchm.org

A wide range of artifacts such as ceramics, bone toothbrushes, and old photographs document a fascinating slice of San Diego's history in this Spanish-style building that once served as a Chinese mission. Of note is the ornate bed that once belonged to a Chinese warlord. In the back garden is a koi pond.

4 Tasende Gallery

MAP N2 ■ 820 Prospect St, La Jolla ■ (858) 454-3691

This gallery presents international contemporary artists. Discover the colorful works of Gaudi-influenced artist Niki de Saint Phalle, the pen-and-ink drawings of Mexico's José Luis Cuevas, and the surrealist paintings of Chilean Roberto Matta, among others.

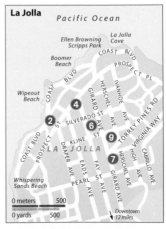

5 Maritime Museum of San Diego

MAP G3 ▪ 1492 N. Harbor Dr ▪ (619) 234-9153 ▪ Open Jun–Aug: 9am–9pm daily; Sep–May: 9am–8pm daily ▪ Adm ▪ www.sdmaritime.org

This fascinating museum pays tribute to the men and ships that so influenced the history and life of San Diego. A range of exhibitions educate and entertain, while several anchored ships can be boarded and explored.

The *Star of India* tall ship, MMSD

6 Alcala Gallery

MAP N3 ▪ 7580 Fay Avenue, Suite 102, La Jolla ▪ (858) 551-5103

Early Californian Impressionist art is well represented here by the land-scapes of Charles A. Fries, Selden Connor Gile, Maurice Braun, and others. The gallery also focuses on ancient pre-Columbian art, Classical and Asian antiquities, and prints.

7 Quint Gallery

MAP N3 ▪ 7547 Girard Avenue, La Jolla ▪ (858) 454-3409

Since 1981, Mark Quint has brought outstanding contemporary artwork to San Diego. Collaborations with collectors, artists, and curators have garnered global acclaim. Exhibited in the 3,000-sq-ft (280-sq-m) space are works by traditional and cutting-edge artists, local and international.

8 Michael J. Wolf Fine Arts

MAP K5 ▪ 363 5th Ave ▪ (619) 702-5388

The oldest gallery in the Gaslamp Quarter features works of emerging US and international contemporary artists. See the urban landscapes of Luigi Rocca, mixed media paintings by Josue Castro, and portraits by Rolling Stone Ronnie Wood.

9 Joseph Bellows Gallery

MAP N3 ▪ 7661 Girard Ave, La Jolla ▪ (858) 456-5620

This intimate gallery showcases important vintage prints and contemporary photographs. Three exhibition areas display photography of a superb quality and host a busy program of themed and solo shows. Both renowned and emerging photographers are represented, and past exhibitions have included work by Ansel Adams, Ave Pildas, Dana Montlack, and Wayne Gudmundson.

10 Spanish Village Art Center

MAP M1 ▪ 1770 Village Pl ▪ (619) 233-9050 ▪ Open 11am–4pm daily ▪ www.spanishvillageart.com

In a Spanish village-like atmosphere adobe houses from the 1935–6 California-Pacific Exposition have been turned into lovely artists' studios, where you can shop or even take a lesson from the artists.

Spanish Village Art Center

🔟 Architectural Highlights

1 San Diego County Administration Center

MAP H3 ■ 1600 Pacific Hwy ■ Open 8am–5pm Mon–Fri

Four architects responsible for San Diego's look collaborated on this civic landmark. What began as a Spanish-Colonial design evolved into a more "Moderne" 1930s style with intricate Spanish tile work and plaster moldings on the tower.

2 Louis Bank of Commerce

Builders of the Hotel del Coronado, the Reid brothers can also take credit for one of the architectural treasures of the Gaslamp Quarter: a stately, four-story twin-towered Victorian structure *(see p12)*. Built in 1888, it was San Diego's first granite building. Of special merit are the ornate bay windows that project from the façade.

3 California Tower and Dome

Bertram Goodhue designed this San Diego landmark for the Panama-California Exposition of 1915–16, using Spanish Plateresque, Baroque, and Rococo details. The geometric tile dome imitates Moorish ceramic work often seen in southern Spain. An iron weather vane in the shape of a Spanish ship tops the 200-ft (61-m) tower *(see p19)*.

California Tower and Dome

The spires of the Mormon Temple

4 Mormon Temple

MAP B1 ■ 7474 Charmant Dr, La Jolla

The temple of the Church of the Latter Day Saints is an ornate, futuristic structure. The golden trumpet-playing angel, Moroni, crowns one of the towers and points the way to Salt Lake City. Interiors are closed to the public.

5 Hotel del Coronado

Designed by James and Merritt Reid in 1887, this hotel was once the largest in the country to be built entirely of wood. Advanced for its time, the hotel had running bathroom water and telephones, as well as a birdcage elevator *(see p28)*.

6 Salk Institute

MAP A1 ■ 10010 N. Torrey Pines Rd ■ (858) 453-4100 ■ Guided tours: noon Mon, Wed & Fri; adm ■ www. salk.edu

At one of the most famous buildings in San Diego *(see p37)*, twin six-story laboratories comprised of teak panels, concrete and glass stand across from each other, separated by a marble courtyard with a channel of water in the middle. Note architect Louis Kahn's use of "interstitial" space: mechanical devices between floors can change laboratory configurations.

El Cortez

MAP K3 ▪ 702 Ash St

This landmark was once the tallest building and most famous hotel in downtown San Diego. A glass elevator once led to the romantic Sky Room. Ornate Spanish details decorate the reinforced concrete structure, which is now a private condo building.

 Geisel Library

MAP B1 ▪ UCSD

Named for famed children's author, Dr. Seuss (see p43), and designed by William Pereira, the library at UCSD (see p37) has tiers of glass walls supported by reinforced concrete cantilevers. Filmmakers have used it as a backdrop for sci-fi shows.

The 1960s Brutalist Geisel Library

 Westfield Horton Plaza

Inside Westfield Horton Plaza is a wonderful hodgepodge of bridges and ramped walkways connecting six staggered levels, embellished with towers and cupolas. Its distinctive sherbet color scheme has been copied on many renovation projects throughout San Diego (see p68).

 Cabrillo Bridge

MAP K1

Built as an entryway to the 1915–16 Panama-California Exposition, this cantilevered and multiple-arched bridge has a 1,500-ft (457-m) span. The best view of the bridge, especially during Christmas, is from the 163 Freeway below.

TOP 10 PUBLIC ART SIGHTS

Guardian of Water

1 Guardian of Water
MAP H3
A 23-ft (70-m) high granite sculpture depicts a pioneer woman.

2 Westfield Horton Plaza Fountain
MAP J5
Flowing water and electric lights were technological breakthroughs in 1909. Plaques honor city notables.

3 Tunaman's Memorial
MAP B5
A bronze sculpture of three tunamen casting their lines.

4 Magic Carpet Ride
MAP D2
The "Cardiff Kook" surfer statue is often elaborately decorated by pranksters.

5 The Cat in the Hat
MAP B1
The Cat in the Hat looks over Dr. Seuss' shoulder in this bronze sculpture.

6 Surfhenge
MAP E3 ▪ Imperial Beach Pier
Surfboards pay tribute to the surf gods.

7 Woman of Tehuantepec
MAP L2 ▪ House of Hospitality
A 1,200-lb (544-kg) piece of limestone is sculpted into an Indian woman.

8 Sun God
MAP B1
A fiberglass bird stretches its wings atop a 15-ft (5-m) concrete arch.

9 Paper Vortex
MAP C5 ▪ San Diego International Airport
A paper airplane is artfully transformed into an origami crane.

10 Homecoming
MAP G4 ▪ Navy Pier, Harbor Drive
A bronze sculpture depicts a sailor and his family in a homecoming embrace.

⭐🔟 Gardens and Nature Reserves

Beach, Torrey Pines State Reserve

① Torrey Pines State Reserve

MAP A1 ▪ 12600 N. Torrey Pines Rd ▪ (858) 755-2063 ▪ Open 7:15am–sunset daily ▪ Parking fee $10–$15

This stretch of California's wild coast *(see p37)* offers a glimpse into an ancient ecosystem. Wildflowers bloom along hiking trails that lead past rare Torrey pines and 300 other endangered species. Viewing areas overlook sandstone cliffs to the beach. Spot quail, mule deer, and coyotes.

② Balboa Park

This landmark destination and heart of San Diego offers an array of superb activities. Visit its gardens and museums for inspiration, to

The Lily Pond at Balboa Park

play sports, or to watch a concert. Although crowded, Sundays are good days to experience the community at leisure *(see pp18–19)*.

③ Spreckels Park

MAP C6 ▪ Coronado

Named after John D. Spreckels *(see p43)*, who donated the land, the park hosts Sunday concerts during the summer as well as art and garden shows. An old-fashioned bandstand, shady trees, green lawns, and picnic tables complete the picture of a small-town community center.

④ Mission Trails Regional Park

MAP F3 ▪ 1 Father Junípero Serra Trail

At one of the country's largest urban parks, hiking and biking trails wind along rugged hills and valleys. The San Diego River bisects the park, and a popular trail leads to the Old Mission Dam. The energetic can hike up Cowles Mountain, San Diego's highest peak at 1,591 ft (485 m).

⑤ Los Peñasquitos Canyon Preserve

MAP E2 ▪ 12020 Black Mountain Rd

Archeologists discovered artifacts of the prehistoric La Jolla culture in this ancient canyon. You can also explore the adobe home of San Diego's first Mexican land grant family. Between two large coastal canyons, trails lead past woodland, oak trees, chaparral, and a waterfall.

⑥ Kate O. Sessions Memorial Park

MAP B3 ▪ 5115 Soledad Rd, Pacific Beach

Named in honor of the mother of Balboa Park *(see p23)*, this peaceful spot, with a terrific view of Mission Bay *(see p53)*, is a popular area for picnics. Take advantage of the ocean breezes to

rediscover kite flying. Walking trails extend 2 miles (3 km) through a canyon lined with native coastal sage.

Mission Bay Park
MAP B4 ▪ 2688 E. Mission Bay Dr

This aquatic wonderland offers every watersport conceivable. You can also bicycle, play volleyball, jog, or nap on the grass. Excellent park facilities include boat rentals, playgrounds, fire rings, and picnic tables (see pp34–5).

Ellen Browning Scripps Park
MAP N2

Broad lawns shaded by palms and Monterey cypress trees stretch along the cliffs from La Jolla Cove to Children's Pool (see p58). Promenades offer stunning views of the cliffs and beach.

Ellen Browning Scripps Park

Embarcadero Marina Park
MAP H6 ▪ Marina Park Way

Join the downtown workers for some fresh air and sunshine. Wide grassy areas and benches give you solitude to enjoy the sweeping views of the harbor. During summer, concerts are held on the lawn.

Tijuana River National Estuarine Research Reserve
MAP E3 ▪ 301 Caspian Way, Imperial Beach

Serene hiking paths wind through fields of wildflowers and plants. More than 300 species of migratory birds stop by at different times of the year. A visitor center offers information to enhance your visit.

TOP 10 SPECTACULAR VIEWS

Boats at Coronado Bridge

1 Point Loma
The breathtaking view from the peninsula's end takes in the city, harbor and Pacific Ocean (see pp30–31).

2 Coronado Bridge
MAP C6
Coronado, downtown, and San Diego harbor sparkle both day and night.

3 Mount Soledad
MAP A2
San Diego's most glorious view takes in Coronado, Point Loma, downtown, the valleys, and Mission Bay.

4 Bertrand at Mr. A's
Planes on approach to Lindbergh Field make dining a visual affair (see p64).

5 Manchester Grand Hyatt San Diego
The 40th-floor lounge offers views of San Diego Bay and Coronado (see p119).

6 Torrey Pines State Reserve
The view down the wind-eroded cliffs and across the Pacific is magnificent.

7 Eddie V's Prime Seafood
Every table here has water views, but the best spot is the upstairs patio with live jazz (see p65).

8 Flying into San Diego
You can almost see what people are having for dinner as you fly in directly over downtown San Diego.

9 Presidio Park
A panoramic view extends from the freeways in Mission Valley below to Mission Bay and the Pacific (see p105).

10 Ferries in San Diego Harbor
On a sunny day, nothing beats a ferry ride on the harbor, gazing at the white sailboats against a blue sky.

🔟 Beaches

The rugged rocks of Windansea Beach

1 Windansea Beach
MAP N3

Legendary among surfers for its shorebreaks, this beach found literary fame as the setting for Tom Wolfe's *The Pumphouse Gang*. The beach gets a little wider south of the "Shack," a local landmark, but those with small children should still take care.

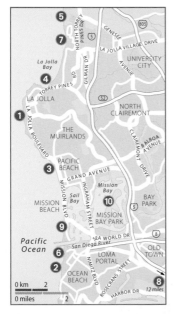

2 Ocean Beach
MAP A4

The laid-back atmosphere of Ocean Beach *(see p93)* attracts not just locals but also some out-of-towners. Surfers usually go out around the pier, and swimmers farther down the beach. There tends to be a strong rip current at the beach, so it is best not to swim out of sight from a lifeguard station. The beach has plenty of facilities, including showers, several picnic tables, and volleyball courts.

3 Pacific Beach

A beach-going spirit fills the air as skateboarders, joggers, and cyclists cruise the promenade parallel to the beach. Chances to people-watch are endless, since Pacific Beach has a reputation for being the place to hang out. Walk out to the Crystal Pier Hotel *(see p120)*, past the bungalows, to watch surfers shooting the curl.

4 La Jolla Shores
MAP Q1

A great family beach, but summer-time gets crowded as sunbathers, Frisbee-throwers, and boogie-boarders spread out along a broad, sandy white strip lapped by gentle surf. Kellogg Park, alongside part of the beach, is a good picnic area for those who forgot their towels. The La Jolla Underwater Ecological Reserve *(see p55)* is just offshore, so divers are usually out in the water.

5 Torrey Pines State Beach
MAP A1

Miles of sandy beaches and secret coves nestle beneath towering sandstone cliffs. During low tide, tide pools offer a glimpse into life under the sea. Torrey Pines is a San Diego favorite because of its lack of crowds, intimacy, and natural beauty. Parking is available at the Torrey Pines State Reserve *(see p50)* or by the gliderport on top of the cliff.

6 Dog Beach
MAP A4 ■ North end of Ocean Beach at San Diego River

Leashes optional! Your dog can run loose to chase after balls, Frisbees, and other dogs with joyous abandon. The beach is open 24 hours, so you can even come here for a midnight swim. Posts with handy plastic bags help you pick up the aftermath.

Pets playing at Dog Beach

7 Black's Beach
MAP A1

This beach is notorious for its nude sunbathers. Access to the beach, which is between Torrey Pines State Beach and La Jolla Shores, is either down an unstable 300-ft (91-m) cliff or via a 1-mile (1.6-km) walk along the beach from either the north or south during low tide. Surfers find the southern end of the beach ideal, as do the hang-gliders who launch off from the cliffs above.

8 Coronado Central Beach
MAP C6

Between the iconic Hotel del Coronado and North Island Naval Air Station, along mansion-lined Ocean Avenue, Coronado's municipal beach has been ranked as one of America's best. Its wide swath of golden sand invites sunbathing, sandcastle building, and family fun. Areas are designated for surfers, swimmers, and fishers, and the north end is for dogs and their humans. US Navy SEALS occasionally pop out of the ocean while training.

9 Mission Beach

At this popular beach *(see p101)*, sunburned, sandy bodies vie for space upon the sand, volleyballs and Frisbees fly overhead, and skateboarders and cyclists try to balance drinks and MP3 players as they careen down the boardwalk. If the beach scene gets overwhelming, Belmont Park *(see p59)* is just a block away.

10 Mission Bay Beaches
MAP B4

Protected from the waves of the Pacific Ocean, 27 miles (43 km) of shoreline, including 19 miles (30 km) of sandy beaches, coves, and inlets, offer idyllic picnic locations. On sunny days, the water is filled with sailboats, kayaks, waterskiers, windsurfers, and rowers. Bike paths wind for miles along the shoreline, and wide grassy areas and ocean breezes make flying kites ideal.

Kayakers at a Mission Bay beach

📟 **Outdoor Activities**

① Horseback Riding
Happy Trails: MAP E3; 2180 Monument Rd; (619) 947-3152; www.ponylandsandiego.com
Guided horseback rides are available on trails, through parks, and on the beach. The South Bay area offers the only beach where you can take an exhilarating ride on the sand and in the waves. There are also pony rides for children, hayrides, and romantic carriage rides.

② Hiking
Hiking is available in every environment imaginable. Los Peñasquitos Canyon Preserve and Mission Trails Regional Park *(see p50)* offer trails of varying difficulty through their canyons and valleys; the trails of Torrey Pines State Reserve and Tijuana River National Estuarine Research Reserve *(see p51)* pass near the ocean. The San Diego Natural History Museum *(see p22)* hosts guided nature tours.

③ Cycling
Bikes & Beyond: MAP C6; 1201 1st St, Coronado; (619) 435-7180
■ **iCommute: dial 511 and say "iCommute"; www.icommutesd.com**
With over 300 miles (483 km) of bikeways, San Diego is a very cycle-friendly city. iCommute's map details bike rides around the city and county, and is available online.

Sailors enjoying the calm waters

④ Sailing and Boating
Seaforth Boat Rentals: MAP B4; 1641 Quivira Rd, Mission Bay; (888) 834-2628
Whether at Mission Bay or the Pacific Ocean, you're bound to see something that floats. Sailing enthusiasts can rent almost any type of boat, some complete with a crew, champagne, and hors d'oeuvres.

⑤ Surfing
San Diego Surfing Academy: (800) 447-7873
San Diego's beaches are famous for surfing. The months with the strongest swells are in late summer and fall, ideally under offshore wind conditions. Designated surfing areas can be found at every beach.

⑥ Swimming
The Plunge: MAP A4; 3115 Ocean Front Walk; (858) 228-9300; adm
Nothing beats an ocean dip, though the temperatures seldom exceed 70° F (21° C) even in the summer. Alternatively, most hotels have pools. The Plunge at the Wave House Athletic Club at Mission Beach is a great public pool.

Cycling in the sunshine

7 Sportfishing
Seaforth Sportsfishing: MAP B4; 1717 Quivira Rd, Mission Bay; (619) 224-3383

Albacore, yellowfin, and dorado are just some of the fish in the offshore waters. Summer and fall are the best months, and half-, full-, and multiple-day trips are all available. A fishing license is not required to fish off the public piers.

8 Golfing
San Diego CVB: MAP J6; (619) 236-1212; www.sandiego.org

With San Diego's perfect climate and amazing views, over 90 public courses and resort hotels offer some of the best golfing in the country. Tee times may be hard to get, so reserve early. The San Diego Convention and Visitors Bureau (CVB) has a golf guide.

A team of golfers at a sand trap

9 Diving
San Diego Ocean Enterprises: MAP B2; 7710 Balboa Ave; (858) 565-6054

The best spots for diving off the coast are the giant kelp forests of Point Loma and the La Jolla Underwater Ecological Reserve. Common sealife includes lobsters and garibaldi – the official state marine fish.

10 Skateboarding
Cheap Rentals: MAP A4; 3689 Mission Blvd; (858) 488-9070; www.cheap-rentals.com

Mission Bay and Pacific Beach are the best areas to enjoy the miles of pathway shared by rollerbladers and joggers. Some areas prohibit skating, so watch out for the signs.

TOP 10 SPECTATOR SPORTS

1 San Diego Chargers
MAP D3 = (619) 280-2121
Try to catch this American Football Conference team playing at its home ground, the Qualcomm Stadium.

2 San Diego Padres
MAP K6 = 100 Park Blvd = (619) 795-5000
Petco Park hosts the National League Padres' baseball team.

3 San Diego State University Aztecs
MAP E4
Take the San Diego Trolley out to Qualcomm Stadium.

4 San Diego Gulls Ice Hockey
MAP B4 = 3500 Sports Arena Blvd = (619) 224-4625
The San Diego Gulls play in the ECHL Premier AA Hockey League.

5 Del Mar Thoroughbred Club
MAP D2 = 2260 Jimmy Durante Blvd, Del Mar = (858) 755-1141
Celebrities and horseracing fans head here to watch the thoroughbreds racing.

6 Hang gliding/Paragliding
Keen hang gliders and paragliders take off from the high ocean cliffs located north of La Jolla (see p56).

7 San Diego Polo Club
MAP E2 = 14555 El Camino Real, Rancho Santa Fe = (858) 481-9217 = Adm
Attend polo matches on Sundays.

8 Golf
Watch the annual golf tournaments at Torrey Pines and La Costa.

9 Mission Bay Park
MAP B3
Mission Bay hosts many boating events.

10 Rodeos
MAP E2
Catch professional rodeo action at Lakeside, Poway, and Ramona.

San Diego Chargers

🔟 Offbeat San Diego

Paragliding at Torrey Pines

machines, video poker, and gaming tables in immense, striking buildings will satisfy the gambler in you.

③ Rent a Harley Davidson
MAP H2 ■ Eagle Rider of San Diego: 2400 Kettner Blvd ■ (619) 446-0022

Born to be wild? Don your jeans and a black leather jacket and rent a bike for a day. You won't be alone: droves of bikers take to the highway, especially on weekends. The back-country of San Diego County is a prime area for powering a Fat Boy, Road King, or Dyna Wide Glide down the road.

④ Biplane Flying
MAP D3 ■ San Diego Air Tours: Montgomery Field ■ (800) 359-2939 ■ www.airtoursofsandiego.com

Two of you sit in the front cockpit of a beautifully restored 1920s biplane wearing helmet and goggles, and soar over beaches, lakes, golf courses, and houses, while the pilot flies behind. The *Beech Belle*, a restored World War II VIP biplane, is great for that special occasion. If you're looking for an extra thrill, the pilot will put you through aerobatic loops and rolls, or you can take the controls in Top Dog Air Combat.

① Paragliding at Torrey Pines
MAP A1 ■ Torrey Pines Gliderport: 2800 Torrey Pines Scenic Dr, La Jolla ■ (858) 452-9858

Soar off the spectacular cliffs of Torrey Pines *(see p50)*. In your first lesson, you'll receive basic instructions followed by 20–30 minutes of gliding with your instructor. If you'd like to watch for a while before making that exhilarating plunge, a viewing area and café sit on the cliff's edge.

② Gambling at Indian Casinos
Barona Resort & Casino: MAP E2; 1932 Wildcat Canyon Rd, Lakeside; (619) 443-2300 ■ Viejas Casino: MAP E2; 5000 Willows Rd, Alpine; (619) 445-5400

Feeling lucky? A dozen tribal casinos promise non-stop Las Vegas-style action and jackpots galore. Starting as a small bingo hall 20 years ago, Indian gaming is now a billion-dollar industry of resort hotels, concert venues, and golf courses. Today, San Diego County has the highest concentration of casinos in the state of California. Thousands of slot

Biplane ride over Torrey Pines

Deer, San Diego Zoo Safari Park

5 Roar and Snore at San Diego Zoo Safari Park

On weekends from May through November, sleep alongside wild animals just as you would in an African game park. Tents that hold up to four persons are provided. Programs include guided discovery hikes and animal encounters, an open-flame grilled dinner, campfire snacks, special late night programs, and a pancake breakfast before a gorgeous sunrise. Reservations are essential (see p99).

6 Tall Ship Adventure Sail

Take a three-hour adventure aboard The Californian, the State of California's official tall ship and a replica of a Gold Rush-era cutter. Passengers can assist in manning the helm, hauling the line, and the end-of-day cannon salute. Crew members tell whaling and battle tales and of San Diego's sailing past. Booking is advised; departure is from the Maritime Museum (see p47).

7 UFO Spotting in East County

MAP F1

Several San Diego groups take UFO (Unidentified Flying Object) sightings seriously. The best places to spot UFOs are in Borrego Springs and Ocotillo Wells. Given San Diego's strong military presence, that saucer in the sky might well be a secret government mission.

8 Diving at Wreck Alley

MAP A4

Just off Mission Beach is the final resting place for the Yukon, a decommissioned Canadian warship, the coastguard cutter Ruby E, and a barge, all deliberately sunk to create an artificial reef. A research tower here collapsed on its own, with its dangling wires and protrusions only adding to the otherworldly, ethereal atmosphere. Thousands of invertebrate marine creatures live here. Charter boats will take you out.

9 Hot-Air Ballooning

MAP E1 ■ California Dreamin': 33133 Vista del Monte Rd, Temecula ■ (800) 373-3359 ■ www.californiadreamin.com

You can watch or take part in inflating a brilliantly colored balloon. Hop in the basket and begin to float over the valleys and hills with a glass of champagne in hand. Balloon rides take flight above the Temecula wine country at sunrise and the Del Mar coastline at sunset.

Hot-air balloon

10 Steam Train Rides

MAP D3 ■ Rohr Park, 4548 Sweetwater Rd, Bonita ■ (619) 397-6197 ■ www.chulavistalivesteamers.org

Chula Vista Live Steamers is run by ordinary people who just happen to love all things steam – lawn mowers, tractors, pumps, cranes, cars, boats, and trains. Dedicated to maintaining the tracks of the Sweetwater & Rohr Park Railroad, the members offer free rides (donations appreciated) on the steam locomotive on the second weekend of each month.

📻🔟 Children's Attractions

Gorilla at San Diego Zoo

1 San Diego Zoo

During seasonal holidays and summer, Dr. Zoolittle presents his entertaining science shows and guest performers delight the crowds. The zoo also offers summer camps and art classes, while special family events are held throughout the year *(see pp20–21)*.

2 Balboa Park Carousel

MAP L2 ■ Balboa Park ■ Adm

Kids will love the carved animals and hand-painted murals of this unique 1910 carousel, right by the zoo. Its Brass Ring game gives riders the chance to win a free turn.

3 LEGOLAND®

Children are fascinated by the 30 million plastic bricks fashioned into famous landmarks and life-sized African animals. In Fun Town, kids can drive electric cars or pilot a helicopter; at the Imagination Zone, they can build robots. Other attractions include a 4-D movie adventure and a waterpark *(see p102)*.

4 Adventure Kids in Egypt at the San Diego Museum of Man

On the museum's second floor, kids dress up as pharaohs and learn about ancient Egypt by building a pyramid, deciphering hieroglyphics, and listening to the god Anubis explain the mummification process. At a re-creation of an archeological dig, children dig through sand for treasure and also learn about identifying an artifact's age *(see p22)*.

5 Marie Hitchcock Puppet Theatre in Balboa Park

MAP L2 ■ Balboa Park ■ (619) 544-9203 ■ Adm ■ www.balboapark puppets.com

Named after the park's beloved and skilled "puppet lady," the Balboa Park Puppet Guild houses a wonderful collection of marionettes and hand, rod, and shadow puppets. The Magic of Ventriloquism, Pinocchio, and Grimm's fairytale classics are some of the shows presented.

Marie Hitchcock Puppet Theatre

6 Harbor Seal-Watching at Children's Pool

MAP N2 ■ Coast Blvd & Jenner St, La Jolla

Children used to swim at this sheltered cove, but harbor seals had much the same idea. The seals are protected by federal law so the beach is now closed, and children must view the entertaining crowds of marine animals swimming and sleeping from behind a rope.

Reuben H. Fleet Science Center

⑦ Reuben H. Fleet Science Center

MAP M1 ■ 1875 El Prado ■ (619) 238-1233 ■ Open 10am–6pm daily (to 8pm Sat) ■ Adm ■ www.rhfleet.org

Science can be fun for all. At Kid City, children aged 2–5 can play with conveyor belts, air chutes, and colorful foam blocks. Older kids go wild building complex structures at Block Busters! and enjoy other hands-on areas. In the Virtual Zone, kids can explore symmetry in time as a video camera records movement.

⑧ Belmont Park

MAP A4 ■ 3190 Mission Blvd ■ (858) 488-1549 ■ Adm for rides

This old-fashioned fun zone keeps the kids entertained for hours. They can board the Giant Dipper roller coaster, take a ride on the Tilt-a-Whirl, and go on an antique carousel; enjoy the Bumper Cars; or climb high above the ground on the challenging Sky Ropes Adventure. For indoor adventures, there's Laser Tag, Laser Maze, rock climbing, and mini golf.

⑨ San Diego Zoo Safari Park

This park has more than 3,000 wild and endangered animals from Africa, Europe, Asia, North and South America, and Australia. Herds of animals roam freely in enclosures that replicate their natural habitats. Compatible animals are mixed, allowing visitors to observe their interactions. Kids will enjoy the safari adventures – ziplines, cheetah runs, and an open-air caravan are among the most popular attractions (see p99).

⑩ Birch Aquarium at Scripps

MAP Q1 ■ 2300 Expedition Way ■ (858) 534-3474 ■ Open 9am–5pm daily ■ Adm ■ www.aquarium.ucsd.edu

Coral reefs, seahorses, octopi, and undulating jellyfish have a high ooh-and-ah factor for kids. The aquarium presents special hands-on activities, scavenger hunts, and craft workshops throughout the year, among more than 30 tanks filled with brilliantly colored fish. Kids love the sea-dragon display and the baby seahorse nursery.

The Giant Dipper at Belmont Park

Performing Arts Venues

1 The Old Globe
MAP L1 ▪ 1363 Old Globe Way
▪ (619) 234-5623 ▪ Check event
schedule ▪ www.theoldglobe.org
Every year 250,000 people attend
performances at the three theaters in
this complex: the 600-seat Old Globe
Theatre, the intimate White Theatre,
and the outdoor Davies Theatre,
which hosts a Shakespeare festival
in the summer.

The Old Globe, built in 1935

2 La Jolla Playhouse
MAP B1 ▪ La Jolla Village Dr
at Torrey Pines Rd, UCSD Campus,
La Jolla ▪ (858) 550-1010
Gregory Peck, Mel Ferrer, and
Dorothy McGuire founded this
theater in 1947. All the Hollywood
greats once performed here. Now
affiliated with UCSD, many plays
that debuted here have gone on to
win the Tony.

3 San Diego Civic Theatre
MAP J4 ▪ 1100 3rd Ave
▪ (619) 570-1100
If you missed the latest Broadway
show, dont worry: chances are the
touring company will perform at this
grand theater. Featuring local talent
and the world's most acclaimed stars,
the San Diego Opera stages four
annual productions here.

4 Lyceum Theatre
MAP J4 ▪ 79 Horton Plaza
▪ (619) 544-1000
Two theaters are part of the San
Diego Repertory Theatre complex:
the 550-seat Lyceum and the 270-
seat Lyceum Space Theatre. Shows
run from the experimental to
multilingual performances and
Shakespeare with a modern slant.
In addition, the theater hosts visiting
companies and art exhibitions.

5 Starlight Bowl
MAP L2 ▪ 2005 Pan American
Plaza ▪ (619) 232-7827 ▪ www.
starlighttheatre.org
The San Diego Civic Light Opera
performs summer Broadway
shows in this idyllic Balboa Park
setting (see pp18–19). It is under a
flight path, so plane-spotters cue
the performers when to freeze.
Audiences good-humoredly accept
the interruptions.

6 Humphrey's Concerts by the Bay
MAP B5 ▪ 2241 Shelter Island Dr,
Shelter Island ▪ (619) 224-3577
From May to October, jazz, rock,
comedy, blues, folk, and world
music are performed in an outdoor
1,350-seat amphitheater next to
San Diego Bay. Special packages
to Humphrey's Restaurant and
Humphrey's Half Moon Inn are
available to patrons (see p119).

Humphrey's Concerts by the Bay

7 Theatre in Old Town
MAP P5 ■ 4040 Twiggs St
■ (619) 337-1525

Only 250 amphitheater-style seats wrap around the stage of this theater in an Old Town barn. Leading local company Cygnet Theatre performs dramas, musicals, and comedies such as *The History Boys*, *A Little Night Music*, and *A Christmas Carol*.

8 Spreckels Theatre
MAP J4 ■ 121 Broadway
■ (619) 235-9500

Commissioned by John D. Spreckels (*see p43*), this Neo-Baroque landmark presents theatrical shows and concerts. Murals, Classical statuary, and an elegant marble lobby give the theater an aura of old San Diego.

Ornate interior, Spreckels Theatre

9 Sleep Train Amphitheatre
MAP E3 ■ 2050 Entertainment Cir, Chula Vista ■ (619) 671-3500

Major pop artists perform from March to October in this notable open-air amphitheater. Great sight lines and giant video screens ensure a good view. There is seating for 10,000 people and the grass can accommodate another 10,000.

10 Copley Symphony Hall
MAP K4 ■ 750 B St ■ (619) 235-0804

Formerly the Fox Theatre, a Rococo-Spanish Renaissance extravaganza built in 1929, this venue was to be destroyed until developers donated it to the San Diego Symphony in 1984. Since restored, the hall hosts excellent classical music concerts.

TOP 10 MOVIES FILMED IN SAN DIEGO

Sands of Iwo Jima, 1949

1 Citizen Kane, 1941
Director and actor Orson Welles used the California Tower and Dome (*see p19*) in Balboa Park as Xanadu.

2 Sands of Iwo Jima, 1949
John Wayne raced up a hill at Camp Pendleton, the setting for the World War II battle in the acclaimed film.

3 Some Like It Hot, 1959
The distinctive structure of the Hotel del Coronado (*see p28*) formed a backdrop for Marilyn Monroe, Jack Lemmon, and Tony Curtis.

4 MacArthur, 1971
Gregory Peck, born in La Jolla in San Diego, played the eponymous general on Silver Strand State Beach.

5 The Stunt Man, 1980
This Peter O'Toole film had several stuntmen jumping off the roof of the city's Hotel del Coronado.

6 Top Gun, 1986
Tom Cruise chatted up Kelly McGillis at the iconic Kansas City Barbecue, in the harbor district.

7 Titanic, 1996
Filmed in an enormous, specially built water tank at Rosarito Beach, Mexico.

8 Almost Famous, 1999
Nothing much had to be changed for the Volkswagen and Birkenstock look of 1970s Ocean Beach (*see p52*).

9 Pearl Harbor, 2000
Kate Beckinsale proved her love for Ben Affleck by bidding him goodbye at the San Diego Railroad Museum in Campo.

10 Traffic, 2000
Along with scenes of San Diego and Tijuana, *Traffic*'s car explosion took place in the judges' parking lot of the Hall of Justice.

⓾ Nightlife

Plush interior of Prohibition

1 Prohibition
MAP K5 ▪ 548 5th Ave ▪ Closed Wed; reservations through website only ▪ Cover charge

A small, intimate jazz bar with perfect martinis and a laid-back crowd that comes for the great music and exceptional service. The bar has the feel of a private members club but it welcomes all.

2 Onyx Room
MAP K5 ▪ 852 5th Ave ▪ (619) 235-6699 ▪ Closed Mon, Wed & Sun ▪ Cover charge Thu–Sat

At this chic basement club, order the cocktail of the month and settle back in a vibrant lounge atmosphere. Upstairs is the Onyx's sister bar Thin, where the unique "engineered" drinks and atmosphere are the epitome of urban cool.

3 Fluxx
MAP J5 ▪ 500 4th Ave ▪ (619) 232-8100 ▪ Open 9pm–2am Thu–Sat ▪ Cover charge and dress code

More of an experience than a club, Fluxx showcases top music events, custom sound and lighting, a huge dance floor, a VIP section, and bottle service. DJs mix up hip-hop, top 40, rock, and electronic sounds.

4 El Dorado Cocktail Lounge
MAP K4 ▪ 1030 Broadway ▪ (619) 237-0550 ▪ Cover charge

This classy boutique martini lounge with Wild West bordello-themed decor offers an amazing variety of entertainment, such as dance parties, DJs, live music, and art shows. The nightly events, top-notch service, and exceptional variety of drinks, including specialty cocktails, draw in the crowds.

5 RoofTop600
MAP K5 ▪ 600 F St ▪ (619) 814-2055 ▪ Cover charge

Located inside the Andaz Hotel, this nightclub is a glittering nightspot with sexy dancers from Thursday to Saturday. An open-air rooftop lounge combines DJ sets with private cabanas and panoramic views of the downtown skyline.

6 Cafe Sevilla
MAP K5 ▪ 353 5th Ave ▪ (619) 233-5979 ▪ Cover charge

This restaurant-nightclub offers everything Latin. Tango and flamenco dinner shows are held in the Spanish restaurant, while instructors teach salsa and samba downstairs. You can practice your moves to the live bands that perform afterward. The basement becomes a Latin/Euro dance club on Friday and Saturday nights.

Latin-style decor at Cafe Sevilla

7 Casbah
MAP H2 ▪ 2501 Kettner Blvd
▪ (619) 232-4355 ▪ Cover charge
Underground alternative rock rules at this grungy club. Famous and future bands turn up the decibels every night. Past headliners have included The Dillinger Escape Plan, The Kills, Futuristic, and Monsieur Periné.

8 The Tipsy Crow
MAP K5 ▪ 770 5th Ave ▪ (619) 338-9300 ▪ Cover charge after 9:30pm Thu & after 8:30pm Fri & Sat
Set in a historic building, the Tipsy Crow occupies three floors. Upstairs are marble fireplaces, tapestries, and a library; on the ground level, a long mahogany bar serves drinks of choice; and the downstairs hosts live music and the Gaslamp Comedy Show.

Exterior of the Tipsy Crow

9 Humphrey's Backstage Live
MAP B5 ▪ 2241 Shelter Island Dr
▪ (619) 224-3577 ▪ Cover charge for most bands
Enjoy a variety of live music nightly at this waterfront lounge with an unbeatable view of the bay. Come early for a terrific happy hour.

10 National Comedy Theatre
MAP C4 ▪ 3717 India St ▪ (619) 295-4999 ▪ Cover charge
Held on Fridays and Saturdays, the National Comedy Theatre's improvisational shows are family-friendly and popular. The audience chooses a game for each show, and decides the winner.

TOP 10 GAY AND LESBIAN VENUES

The main dancefloor at Spin

1 Spin
MAP C4 ▪ 2028 Hancock St ▪ (619) 294-9590
Three floors of bars and a dance club.

2 Cheers of San Diego
MAP D4 ▪ 1839 Adams Ave ▪ (619) 298-3269
This dependably divey beer and wine bar has been in business since 1982.

3 The Brass Rail
MAP C4 ▪ 3796 5th Ave ▪ (619) 298-2233
San Diego's oldest gay bar.

4 Urban Mo's Bar & Grill
MAP C4 ▪ 308 University Ave ▪ (619) 491-0400
Rowdy, hetero-friendly drag club.

5 Pecs
MAP C4 ▪ 2046 University Ave ▪ (619) 296-0889
Gay Harley-Davidson enthusiasts frequent this popular bar.

6 The Gossip Grill
MAP C4 ▪ 1440 University Ave ▪ (619) 260-8023
A lesbian restaurant and bar with a sensual atmosphere and great food.

7 Number One Fifth Ave
MAP C4 ▪ 3845 5th Ave ▪ (619) 299-1911
Video bar, pool table, and patio.

8 Numbers
MAP D4 ▪ 3811 Park Blvd ▪ (619) 294-7583
Pool tables and two dance floors.

9 Rich's
MAP C4 ▪ 1051 University Ave ▪ (619) 295-2195
Dancing go-go boys and girls.

10 Lips San Diego
MAP D4 ▪ 3036 El Cajon Blvd ▪ (619) 295-7900
Drag shows and crowded Sunday brunches, with a cover charge.

🔟 Restaurants

Dining room with a view, Bertrand at Mr. A's

① Bertrand at Mr. A's
MAP J1 ▪ 2550 5th Ave,
12th Floor ▪ (619) 239-1377 ▪ $$

For casually elegant dining with a dazzling view, this restaurant with friendly staff is hard to beat. The seasonal menu of New American dishes is inspired by contemporary French-Mediterranean cuisine. Popular choices include sautéed Alaskan halibut with scallops and a trio of vegetarian creations.

② Island Prime
MAP C5 ▪ 880 Harbor Island Dr
▪ (619) 298-6802 ▪ $$$

Presided over by chef Deborah Scott, scrumptious New American cuisine includes fresh seafood, prime steaks, mouthwatering "Deborah's Compositions," and fine wines. The C Level bar (with a happy hour) offers appetizers and more filling fare.

③ El Agave Tequileria
Ancient Mexican and Spanish spices and traditions make for a unique Mexican dining experience. Shrimp, sea bass, and the filet mignon prepared with goat's cheese and a dark tequila sauce are heavenly. Mole, the distinctive blending of spices, garlic, and sometimes chocolate, is a specialty. There are some 150 tequila selections (see p89).

④ The Marine Room
MAP P2 ▪ 2000 Spindrift Dr,
La Jolla ▪ (866) 644-2351 ▪ $$$

Dine on exciting, romantic global cuisine derived from French classics. If you're not that hungry and would like to enjoy the sunset, try hors d'oeuvres in the lounge.

⑤ Sushi Ota
Don't be fooled by the modest exterior: this is possibly the city's most cherished restaurant for an authentic Japanese experience and all things sushi, as proven by the many Japanese patrons. The restaurant is also famous for its sea urchin dishes (see p105).

⑥ Baci Ristorante
MAP B3 ▪ 1955 W. Morena Blvd
▪ (619) 275-2094 ▪ $$

Classic Italian cuisine is presented in this subtly modern restaurant with Old World charm. The menu includes creative specials, as well as traditional veal, seafood, and pasta dishes. The wine list is extensive.

⑦ The Prado at Balboa Park
MAP L1 ▪ 1549 El Prado, Balboa Park
▪ (619) 557-9441 ▪ $$

Hand-painted ceilings, glass sculptures, and whimsical artwork adorn this atmospheric restaurant. A large terrace overlooks the gardens of Balboa Park. A variety of margaritas and drinks from around South America complement an excellent cuisine best described as Latin and Italian fusion.

8 Filippi's Pizza Grotto
MAP H3 ▪ 1747 India St ▪ (619) 232-5095 ▪ $

At this Little Italy favorite, the dim lights, red-checkered tablecloths, and hundreds of Chianti bottles hanging from the ceiling haven't changed in decades. Enter through the Italian deli in front to get to the authentic dishes on offer.

9 Eddie V's Prime Seafood
Views of La Jolla Cove loom from every table of this casually upscale restaurant. Mouth-melting seafood, selections from the oyster bar, and comfort-food sides pair with wines from the highly praised cellar. Live jazz plays nightly on the upper level patio *(see p105)*.

Interior of Eddie V's Prime Seafood

10 Emerald Chinese Seafood Restaurant
MAP D3 ▪ 3709 Convoy St, Kearny Mesa ▪ (858) 565-6888 ▪ $$

San Diego's best Chinese restaurants are found in Kearny Mesa. The Asian community packs into this large dining room to enjoy lunchtime dim sum and fresh, simple but exquisitely prepared seafood dishes at dinner.

TOP 10 ROMANTIC RESTAURANTS

Refined dining at 1500 Ocean

1 1500 Ocean
Excellent service and elegant offerings at this impressive spot *(see p97)*.

2 Mille Fleurs
A charming French restaurant with top service and a great wine list *(see p105)*.

3 Chez Loma
Delicious French cuisine here creates the ingredients for romance *(see p97)*.

4 Old Venice
MAP B5 ▪ 2910 Cañon St ▪ (619) 222-5888 ▪ $$
A casually elegant venue that's not too pricey in Point Loma.

5 BiCE
MAP J5 ▪ 425 Island Ave ▪ (619) 239-2423 ▪ $$
Authentic Italian dishes are served in this modern, elegant restaurant.

6 The WineSellar & Brasserie
MAP D2 ▪ 9550 Waples St, Suite 115 ▪ (858) 450-9557 ▪ $$$
A delightful brasserie with excellent wine tasting.

7 Candelas on the Bay
MAP C6 ▪ 1201 1st St, Coronado ▪ (619) 435-4300 ▪ $$
Mexican nouvelle cuisine in a chic setting. Seafood is the specialty here.

8 The Marine Room
Haute cuisine, candlelight, and soft music arouse the senses *(see p64)*.

9 George's at the Cove
MAP P2 ▪ 1250 Prospect St ▪ (858) 454-4244 ▪ $$$
The most popular place to propose in San Diego.

10 Primavera Ristorante
MAP C6 ▪ 932 Orange Ave ▪ (619) 435-0454 ▪ $$
Specialties like *osso bucco* can melt hearts at this slice of Northern Italy.

For a key to restaurant price ranges see p83

Cafés and Bars

1 Cafe-Bar Europa – The Turquoise
MAP A3 ▪ 873 Turquoise St ▪ (858) 488-4200

Reminiscent of the bars of Bohemian Europe, this Pacific Beach café exudes tradition in a high-speed world. You can even philosophize over a glass of absinthe. Tapas are the featured fare in the restaurant, and live entertainment is scheduled most nights.

2 La Sala
MAP N2 ▪ La Valencia Hotel: See p118 ▪ No dis. access

Sitting in the hotel's lobby lounge amid Spanish mosaics, hand-painted ceilings and murals, red-tiled floors, and huge palms is like being in a Spanish palace. Order a drink and gaze out at the ocean; a pianist plays in the evening. On sunny days, take advantage of the outside tables.

3 Habano's Café & Cigar Lounge
MAP B4 ▪ 3111 Hancock St ▪ (619) 692-0696

Buy a cigar from the huge stock in the walk-in humidor, then light up in a rustic setting with big, comfortable furniture or on the patio. There are also craft beers, espresso, tapas, and panini. Bands play on weekends.

4 Bean Bar
MAP K6 ▪ 1068 K St ▪ (503) 358-8554

Baristas make your coffee from the finest beans at this East Village neighborhood café, small in size but big on quality. Service is friendly, beverages are diligently prepared, and the proprietors firmly believe in direct trade.

Lestat's Coffee House

5 Lestat's Coffee House
MAP D4 ▪ 3343 Adams Ave ▪ (619) 282-0437

Named after the character in Anne Rice's vampire novels, this café in a hip spot serves coffee and pastries 24 hours a day. Local bands entertain in the evening. There's free Wi-Fi, too.

6 The Field Irish Pub
MAP K5 ▪ 544 5th Ave ▪ (619) 232-9840

Literally imported from Ireland, the wood walls, flooring, decorations, and assorted curios were shipped over and reassembled. Even the bartenders and waitresses are the real thing, not to mention the Guinness. Grab a sidewalk seat on Fifth Avenue or try for a window seat upstairs. The pub food is also great.

St. Patrick's Day at the Field Irish Pub

7 Twiggs Bakery & Coffee House

MAP D4 ▪ 4590 Park Blvd ▪ (619) 296-0616

Enjoy a latte and a snack in this fun café. It's packed all day with locals. On the second and fourth Mondays of each month, you'll find poetry readings being held here.

8 Top of the Hyatt

Window seats at this bar in the Manchester Grand Hyatt hotel are at a premium at sunset, offering breathtaking views of the bay, Coronado, Point Loma, and the jets over Lindbergh Field. Dark woods exude a sedate, plush atmosphere, with drink prices to match *(see p119)*.

Elegant interior of the Top of the Hyatt

9 Wet Stone Wine Bar & Café

MAP J4 ▪ 1927 4th Ave ▪ (619) 255-2856

Chef/owner Christian Gomez serves bold dishes in an intimate, eclectic space with tropical plants, against a soundtrack of sultry rhythms. Carefully selected wines are available by the glass or bottle.

10 Waterfront Bar & Grill

MAP H3 ▪ 2044 Kettner Blvd ▪ (619) 232-9656

San Diego's oldest tavern opened shortly after Prohibition ended. Customers at this basic watering hole ranged from laborers to lawyers, and the present clientele is still diverse. Business is brisk, the bar is fully stocked, and burgers and light fare are on the menu.

TOP 10 BREAKFAST SPOTS

Outdoor seating at The Cottage

1 The Cottage
Enjoy the freshly-baked cinnamon rolls and Belgian waffles *(see p101)*.

2 Café 222
MAP J5 ▪ 222 Island Ave ▪ (619) 236-9902 ▪ $
Try pumpkin waffles and French toast.

3 Brockton Villa
Start the morning with crêpes, omelets, or a "tower of bagel" *(see p104)*.

4 Crown Room
MAP C6 ▪ Hotel del Coronado
The room is legendary, the Sunday feast amazing *(see p28)*.

5 Hash House A Go Go
MAP C4 ▪ 3628 5th Ave ▪ (619) 298-4646 ▪ No dis. access ▪ $
Locals vote this hip, award-winning café the best breakfast spot in town.

6 Hob Nob Hill
MAP J2 ▪ 2271 1st Ave ▪ (619) 239-8176 ▪ $
Waffles, omelets, and pancakes.

7 Broken Yoke Café
MAP A3 ▪ 1851 Garnet Ave ▪ (858) 270-0045 ▪ $
Choose from 30 varieties of omelets.

8 Kono's Café
MAP A3 ▪ 704 Garnet Ave ▪ (858) 483-1669 ▪ No credit cards ▪ No dis. access ▪ $
Join the line for banana pancakes and breakfast burritos.

9 Richard Walker's Pancake House
MAP J5 ▪ 520 Front St ▪ (619) 231-7777 ▪ $
More than 100 items are offered here.

10 The Mission
MAP A3 ▪ 3795 Mission Blvd ▪ (858) 488-9060 ▪ $
Breakfast is served until 3pm in this funky "Chino-Latino" café.

For a key to restaurant price ranges see p83

🔟 Stores and Shopping Centers

① Nordstrom
MAP J5 ■ 103 Horton Plaza

Holding an almost cult-like status among shopping fanatics, "Nordies" remains as popular as ever for its vast clothing selection and impressive shoe department. Belying the plush surroundings, this department store can be quite affordable. Of course, there is always the personal shopper who will help you out in the designer section. The Nordstrom Café is popular for lunch, serving soups, sandwiches, pasta dishes, and salads.

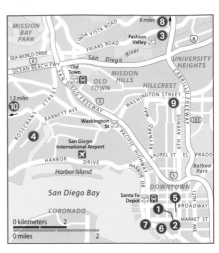

② Westfield Horton Plaza
MAP J5 ■ 4th Ave & Broadway ■ (619) 239-8180

Macy's and Nordstrom department stores serve as anchors to this festive shopping experience, a destination in its own right. Designed as an amusement park for shoppers, ramps lead past staggered shopping

Westfield Horton Plaza

levels that hold more than 130 specialty shops, a few restaurants, and movie theaters. The Plaza's landmark is the 1907 Jessop's Clock, a 21-ft- (6.4-m-) high timepiece with 20 dials that display the time in all parts of the world (see p78).

③ Fashion Valley
MAP C4 ■ 7007 Friars Rd

This ritzy shopping center contains six major department stores, including Neiman Marcus and Nordstrom, as well as 200 specialty boutiques. Tiffany & Co., MAC cosmetics, and Louis Vuitton are just a few of the stores found here. The San Diego Trolley conveniently stops in the parking lot.

④ Liberty Station
MAP B5 ■ 2640 Historic Decatur Rd

Formerly the Naval Training Center, this waterfront compendium of Spanish Colonial-Revival buildings now welcomes shoppers with its grocery stores, art galleries, and wine bars. Monthly art walks and live entertainment are free, as is parking.

5 The Wine Bank
MAP K5 ▪ 363 5th Ave
▪ (619) 234-7487

A regular clientele of wine connoisseurs frequent this intimate Gaslamp business. Hundreds of offerings from California and the rest of the world are found on two floors. The expertise of its wine professionals will help in your selection of fine wines in all price ranges. Call for the latest wine tasting schedule.

6 Girard Avenue & Prospect Street
MAP N2

These intersecting streets in La Jolla are synonymous with upscale shopping and high-end art galleries. If you're seeking an expensive look, chic clothing boutiques and Italian shoe stores will happily oblige. The gorgeous displays in the home decor shops will give you great ideas to take home. In the breezy arcades, don't miss the one-of-a-kind shops and beachwear boutiques.

7 Seaport Village
MAP H5 ▪ 849 W. Harbor Dr
▪ (619) 235-4014 ▪ Open Sep–May: 10am–9pm; Jun–Aug: 10am–10pm

If you're looking for souvenirs or that unusual knick-knack for the shelf, this is the right place. You'll find kites, magnets, gifts for left-handed people, and T-shirts galore. The Village's superb location along San Diego's waterfront will keep you occupied.

The waterfront Seaport Village

8 REI
MAP C2 ▪ 5556 Copley Dr
▪ (858) 279-4400

To participate in San Diego's outdoor life, you might need some sports equipment. This store has it all, including rentals of camping gear, snowshoes, and tents, as well as a full-service bike shop. You can also take bike lessons, enjoy lectures, and sign up for photography classes.

Secondhand store on Fifth Avenue

9 University and Fifth Avenues
MAP C4

In Uptown, near the intersection of University and Fifth Avenues, the predominately gay and lesbian Hillcrest neighborhood is a haven of fun and enticing shops, cafés, restaurants, and bars. Bookshops, resale wear, and vinyl record stores are among the independent businesses.

10 Newport Avenue
MAP A4

This is not just the main road through town; it is also one big blast into the past before the street hits the beach. You can pick up anything from Arts and Crafts-era pottery to tie-dye T-shirts. Street parking is available.

🔟 San Diego for Free

Seals lying around the Children's Pool in La Jolla

① Whales, Dolphins, and Seals

In season, you can often see migrating whales while staring out to sea. The same is true for dolphins, especially in the Encinitas area. Harbor seals can be seen lazing around the Children's Pool in La Jolla *(see p58)*, for which the normal fee is waived on Tuesdays.

② Nature Trails

Explore the miles of hiking trails at the Mission Trails Regional Park (www.mtrp.org) and the Torrey Pines State Preserve *(see p50)*. The latter is also prime bird-watching territory. All of San Diego's beaches and parks are great for picnics.

③ Timken Museum of Art

MAP L1 ■ 1500 El Prado, Balboa Park ■ (619) 239-5548 ■ www.timkenmuseum.org

Admittance is free to this impressive and important collection of Russian icons, Parisian tapestries, European Old Masters, American works, and other fine art. The permanent collection includes Bruegel, Rubens, Vermeer, and *Saint Bartholomew* – San Diego's only Rembrandt painting *(see p22)*.

Timken Museum of Art

⑨ Park at the Parks

Park for free and enter for free at the city's glorious parks with year-round blossoms and playgrounds for the kids. Centerpiece Balboa Park is by far the urban favorite, while Old Town is full of history and aquatic Mission Bay Park is great for families. Ethereal skies and sands at Anza-Borrego are also free.

⑤ International Cottages

MAP L1 ■ 1549 El Prado, Balboa Park ■ (619) 234-0739 ■ Open four hours between noon and 5pm Sunday ■ www.sdhpr.org

More than 30 countries are represented within the historic 1935 cottages of Balboa Park's House of Hospitality. At 2pm, on a rotating basis, member houses epitomize their countries through song, dance, or other means *(see p19)*.

⑥ Shakespeare Readings

MAP H5 ■ Upstart Crow Bookstore & Coffee House, 835 West Harbor Drive, Suite C ■ (619) 232-4855 ■ 6:45–8pm 1st Tue ■ www.sandiego shakespearesociety.org

Everyone is welcome to join the San Diego Shakespeare Society to participate in or listen with other aficionados to works by the Bard.

Walking Tours
(619) 231-7463 ■ www.
walkabout-int.org/wabt.html
Walkabout International leads
free tours in and around San Diego.
Some walks go through decorated
neighborhoods, while others focus
on architecture. Standard walks take
place in Mission Bay, Shelter Island,
Balboa Park, and Mission Hills.

8 **Gaze at the Stars**
View the night sky at the
Reuben H. Fleet Science Center *(see
p59)* in Balboa Park. Visitors can stargaze for free on the first Wednesday
of every month, starting at 8pm,
through giant telescopes from the
San Diego Astronomy Association.

Spreckel's Organ Pavilion

4 **Art and Music**
Spreckels Organ Society: (619)
702-8138; www.spreckelsorgan.org
There are gallery openings most
weekends and a monthly art walk at
Liberty Station. Free concerts are also
held during the summer; many take place
at beaches and parks throughout
summer, including performances by
the renowned Spreckels Organ Society.
For listings, check www.sandiego.org.

10 **59-Mile Scenic Drive**
www.sandiego.org
This three-hour drive winds through
the city's neighborhoods and offers
a plethora of memorable views,
from the coastline, the bay, and the
downtown skyline, to the bordering
mountains, and even Mexico. The
drive can also be spread out over
several days.

TOP 10 MONEY-SAVING TIPS

The free tram in Balboa Park

1 Ride Balboa Park's free daily tram
from Inspiration Point parking lot to
El Prado attractions.
www.balboapark.org/visit/parking

2 Purchase the Compass Card day or
multiday pass for easy riding across
buses and trolleys.
www.511sd.com/compass

3 Save money and skip lots of lines at
theme parks and zoos with CityPass.
**www.citypass.com/southern-
california**

4 Visit many museums and San Diego
Zoo with Balboa Park Explorer Pass.
www.balboapark.org/explorer

5 Parking is free on most city side
streets, but check signs for time limits.

6 Both the downtown and La Jolla locations of the Museum of Contemporary
Art *(see p46)* are free on the third
Thursday of every month, from 5–7pm.
www.mcasd.org

7 Check online site Groupon for deals
on dining, attractions, and tours.
www.groupon.com/local/san-diego

8 Published weekly, *San Diego Reader*
lists free and cheap events and deals.
www.sandiegoreader.com

9 ArtsTix
Pick up half-price theater tickets at
the ArtsTix kiosk in front of Westfield
Horton Plaza.
www.sdartstix.com

10 Morley Field Sports Complex
Join free or inexpensive sports
activities, from jogging and cycling, to
archery, basketball, and boccie.
**www.balboapark.org/in-the-park/
morley-field-sports-complex
www.sandiego.gov/park-and-
recreation/centers/recctr/morley**

🔟 Festivals

1 Mardi Gras
Gaslamp Quarter ■ Feb/Mar

Be quick to grab the strings of beads thrown off the floats at the Masquerade Parade. The parade begins in the afternoon at Fifth Avenue, and the music and revelry carry on until the early morning. The food booths serve up New Orleans-style Cajun food.

2 St. Patrick's Day Parade
Mar

A grand parade of marching bands, bagpipes, community organizations, horses, and school groups begins at Sixth and Juniper. Afterward, an Irish festival takes place at Balboa Park with Irish dancers, lots to eat, green beer, and fun for the entire family.

3 Cinco de Mayo
May

North of the Mexican border, commemorating the French defeat by Mexican troops is a serious business. Restaurants overflow, the Old Town State Historic Park sponsors folkloric ballet performances and mariachi bands, and the historic Gaslamp Quarter hosts a musical street fair.

Fireworks marking the Fourth of July

4 Fourth of July Fireworks and Parades
Jul

Nearly every San Diego community has its own July 4th festivities, such as fireworks, surfing contests, parades, and street festivals. Since the ban of home fireworks, commercial fireworks shows are the way to go. The biggest show in the county is held over San Diego Harbor.

St. Patrick's Day Parade

5 Comic-Con International
Convention Center ■ Late Jul

Comic-Con draws more than 150,000 devotees over several days and literally bursts out of the huge San Diego Convention Center. Tickets sell out super-fast for this wildly popular all-things-comic-and-then-some gathering. Celebrity guests, panels, retailers, games, anime, film screenings, and fringe events line the program.

6 Lesbian and Gay Parade and Festival
End Jul

San Diego's gay community hits the streets in celebration of diversity. The iconic parade begins at Fifth Avenue and Laurel in Hillcrest and moves to Balboa Park, where live bands, food booths, and a party atmosphere prevail. Outrageous costumes are the rule of the day.

Dancer at Cinco de Mayo celebrations

Halloween Festivals & Haunted Houses
Gaslamp Quarter & Balboa Park ■ Oct ■ Adm

Your worst nightmares may come true at the historic 1889 Haunted Hotel, which features ghouls, a clown asylum, and a haunted subway station. The Chamber and Haunted Trails of Balboa Park will terrify you.

 Mother Goose Parade
El Cajon ■ Sun before Thanksgiving

Floats, equestrian units, and marching bands make up part of the 200 entries in the largest single-day event in San Diego County, attended by about 400,000 people. A tradition since 1947, the parade revolves around a celebration of children.

Mother Goose Parade

 Christmas on the Prado
Balboa Pk ■ First Fri & Sat of Dec

Balboa Park launches the Christmas season by opening its doors to the community. Museums are free after 5pm, carolers sing, and food booths are set up. The park is closed to traffic, but shuttles reach the outer parking lots. Dress warmly.

 Boat Parades of Lights
Dec

Yachts and sailboats vie for the title of best decorated in Mission Bay and the San Diego Harbor. The best viewing areas for the Mission Bay parade are at Crown Point and Fiesta Island; for the San Diego Harbor Parade, head to the Embarcadero.

TOP 10 FAIRS AND GATHERINGS

1 Ocean Beach Kite Festival
Ocean Beach ■ Mar
A kite competition with prizes and demonstrations on the beach.

2 Avocado Festival
Fallbrook ■ Apr
Special tours, 50 food booths, and awards for best dishes draw big crowds.

3 San Diego County Fair
Del Mar ■ Jun ■ Adm
Animals, rides, food, and music.

4 A Taste of Gaslamp
Gaslamp Quarter ■ Jun ■ Adm
A self-guided tour passes restaurants displaying their kitchen samplings.

5 Mainly Mozart Festival
Apr–Jun ■ Adm
Concerts at San Diego and Tijuana feature works by the wunderkind and his contemporaries.

6 US Open Sand Castle Competition
Imperial Beach ■ Aug
Competitors build the most complex and imaginative sand castles.

7 Summerfest
Aug
Classical music and modern compositions in La Jolla, with artists and ensembles from around the world.

8 Julian Fall Apple Harvest
Mid-Sep–mid-Oct
Music, apple cider, and apple pies in a charming mountain town.

9 Cabrillo Festival
Cabrillo National Monument ■ End Sep ■ Adm
Soldiers re-enact the Cabrillo landing, and performers showcase Native American, Aztec, and Mayan dances.

10 Fleet Week
Sep/Oct
Navy ship tours and air and sea parades honor the military.

San Diego County Fair performers

San Diego
Area by Area

View across the marina toward the
waterfront and its high-rises

TOP10 Downtown San Diego

Scarcely a generation ago, one drove through downtown San Diego with the windows rolled up, past derelict tattoo parlors and sleazy porn palaces. But it has transformed into a first-class destination for visitors and a trendy area for residents. There are restaurants, art galleries, festivals, performing arts centers, museums, and a sports stadium. The atmosphere is strictly Southern Californian: a blend of urban energy and laid-back priorities. From the edge of the Embarcadero to the beautifully restored Gaslamp Quarter, downtown is a great place to have fun in.

San Diego Museum of Man in Balboa Park

AREA MAP OF DOWNTOWN SAN DIEGO

Downtown

Around the bay

0 meters 500
0 yards 500

Walkway on the Embarcadero

1 Embarcadero

For those arriving by ship or train, the Embarcadero is San Diego's front door. Passengers disembark from gleaming white cruise ships tied up at B Street Pier or pass through a 1915 train depot. But the Embarcadero is an attraction in itself. Pedestrian-friendly walkways pass historic ships, museums, shopping centers, and parks. Serious and quirky public artworks and a harbor filled with maritime life define this lively district (see pp14–15).

2 Gaslamp Quarter

In the mid-19th century, the Gaslamp Quarter was the heart of a new city, but within 50 years it had fallen prey to gambling halls, opium dens, and houses of prostitution, and within another 50 years, it had become a broken-down slum. Now the Gaslamp Quarter sparkles as it looks to a brilliant future. During the day, the gloriously restored buildings attract history buffs and shoppers. By night, crowds dine in fashionable restaurants, listen to music, or sip drinks (see pp12–13).

The historic Gaslamp Quarter

3 Balboa Park and San Diego Zoo

Home to the world-famous San Diego Zoo, 15 unique museums, theaters, countless recreational opportunities, and exquisite landscaping, Balboa Park creates an indelible impression. Year round, vibrant flowers bloom in profusion and pepper tree groves and grassy expanses provide idyllic spots for picnicking. Allow a minimum of a few days to enjoy the park's many attractions (see pp18–23).

①	**Top 10 Sights** see pp77–9
①	**Places to Eat** see p83
①	**Shopping** see p80
①	**Cruising the Bay** see p82
①	**Museum Shops** see p81

0 km 2
0 miles 2

Central Library, East Village

4 East Village
MAP L5

Formerly a Victorian village that fell into neglect but survived as a warehouse district and artist colony, this area is now very fashionable. Petco Park, home to the San Diego Padres baseball team (see p55), is the neighborhood's major focal point. Check out the 1909 Western Metal Supply building: architects incorporated the vintage building into the stadium's structure. A state-of-the-art Central Library and a Children's Museum are located here.

5 Westfield Horton Plaza
When it opened in 1985, developers hoped this unique shopping center (see p68) would help revive a declining area. It was an immediate hit – people loved the Plaza's inward-facing design, tiered shopping levels, and the 43 unusual colors of paint on its walls. Over several city blocks, the plaza features more than 130 shops, movie theaters, and stage shows at the Lyceum Theatre (see p60). Adjacent to Westfield Horton Plaza is the Balboa Theatre (see p13). Built as a cinema in 1924, it now offers live shows.

6 Little Italy
MAP J3

This revitalized neighborhood is one of San Diego's oldest. Genoese fishing families were the first Italians to settle along the waterfront in the 1860s. Along with Portuguese immigrants, they founded San Diego's prosperous tuna industry. Little Italy, sometimes known as Middletown, is now a fashionable address. While retaining its Bohemian character, restaurants, galleries, design stores, and a Saturday market line its streets.

7 Asian Pacific Historic District
MAP J5

An eight-block area that overlaps part of the Gaslamp Quarter marks the former center of San Diego's Asian community. The Chinese came to San Diego after the California Gold Rush and found fishing and construction work; others ran opium dens and gambling halls. Japanese and Filipino communities followed. This is the home of Chinese New Year celebrations, a farmers' market, and an Asian bazaar. Join a walking tour at the Chinese Historical Museum (see p46), and look for Asian architectural flourishes on the buildings.

8 Marston House
MAP K1 ■ 3525 7th Ave ■ (619) 298-3142 ■ Open for docent-led tours only: half-hourly tours start at 10am; last tour begins at 4:30pm ■ Adm

This fine Arts and Crafts house, built in 1905, is open to the public as a museum. The exterior combines

---

THE FOUNDING OF MODERN SAN DIEGO

When entrepreneur Alonzo Horton arrived in a burgeoning San Diego in 1867, he believed that a new city could prosper in this location. He bought 960 acres and sold and even gave away lots to people. When you walk the Gaslamp Quarter, note the short blocks and lack of alleys, created due to the opinion that corner lots were worth more and alleys only accumulated trash.

elements of Victorian and English Tudor styles, while the interior offers expansive hallways and intimate living spaces adorned with Mission-style furnishings, fine pottery, paintings, and textiles by craftsman artisans. The museum is operated by the San Diego Historical Society.

⑨ Martin Luther King Promenade
MAP H5

Planner Max Schmidt used the idea of functional public art to create this 1/4-mile (0.4-km) promenade along Harbor Drive. Described as a "serape" of colors, textures, and waterworks, the promenade celebrates a multicultural heritage. Granite stones bear quotes by civil-rights leader Dr. Martin Luther King.

Martin Luther King Promenade

⑩ Museum of Contemporary Art
MAP H4 ■ 1001 & 1100 Kettner Blvd ■ (858) 454-3541 ■ Open 11am–5pm Thu–Tue (11am–7pm 3rd Thu each month) ■ Docent-led tours: 6pm 3rd Thu each month (free), 2pm Sat & Sun ■ Adm

This two-building downtown location of the museum in La Jolla (see p36) presents rotating art exhibits, as well as selected pieces from the permanent collection. At the entrance is the 18-ft (5.4-m) *Hammering Man at 3,110,527*, a steel and aluminum sculpture by Jonathan Borofsky. The museum also hosts lectures and workshops, and there is a themed gallery tour at the free opening on the third Thursday evening each month.

A DAY WALKING AROUND DOWNTOWN

▶ MORNING

Start at the **Santa Fe Depot** (see p15). Walk right on Broadway, cross the RR tracks, and walk two blocks to Harbor Drive. Turn right and head to the **Maritime Museum of San Diego** (see p47). Check out the exhibits and climb aboard the *Star of India*. Walk back down Harbor Drive to the ticket booth for harbor tours. A narrated harbor cruise brings you close to the naval facilities. Next, spend an hour or so aboard the **USS *Midway*** at the **USS Midway Museum** (see pp16–17). Finish your morning with lunch at the **Fish Market**, N. Harbor Drive (619-232-3474).

AFTERNOON

Continue down Harbor Drive to **Seaport Village** (see p14) and stay on the sidewalk until you reach a crossing. Turn left; walk up the street past the **Manchester Grand Hyatt Hotel**, across Harbor Drive and the trolley tracks. Walk onto the **Martin Luther King Promenade**, which stretches past beautiful downtown apartment revitalizations. At the Convention Center trolley stop, turn left, then left again on J St. On J and 3rd, stop by the **San Diego Chinese Historical Museum** (see p46). Turn left on 3rd and right on Island; you'll pass the historic **Horton Grand Hotel**. At 4th, visit the **William Heath Davis House** (see p12). One block farther is the heart of the **Gaslamp Quarter**. Pick up a sundae at **Ghirardelli Soda Fountain** at 631 5th Street.

See map on pp76–7 ⬅

Shopping

1 Goorin Bros. Hat Shop
MAP K5 ■ 631 5th Ave ■ (619) 450-6303

Established in 1895, this is the place for serious lovers of quality headgear of all shapes and styles, catering to both men and women.

2 The Wine Bank
MAP K6 ■ 363 5th Ave, Suite 100 ■ (619) 234-7487

Come here for expert staff and two floors of North American and international wines in all price ranges.

3 Urban Outfitters
MAP K5 ■ 665 5th Ave ■ (619) 231-0102

This one-stop clothing shop for the young and trendy never lags behind the latest styles. Their original home accessories with an urban edge are true conversation pieces.

4 Blick Art Materials
MAP H3 ■ 1844 India St ■ (619) 687-0050

Blick stocks sketch pads, watercolor sets, papers and canvases, journals, and just about any type of painting, drawing, or writing implement.

5 Vocabulary
MAP H3 ■ 414 W. Cedar St ■ (619) 203-4066

This intimate Little Italy boutique sells apparel for men and women, baby items, home decor, paper goods, and accessories and gifts.

Interior of Vocabulary

6 Chuck Jones Gallery
MAP K6 ■ 232 5th Ave ■ (619) 294-9880

American Pop artworks are on sale here in a gallery setting. Featured artists include Chuck Jones, Dr. Seuss, Charles Schulz, and Tom Everhart.

7 Bubbles Boutique
MAP K6 ■ 226 5th Ave ■ (619) 236-9003

A chic boutique selling trendy casualwear, luxurious pajamas, hand-crafted bath products, and a great selection of gifts and accessories.

8 The Cuban Cigar Factory
MAP K5 ■ 551 5th Ave ■ (619) 238-2496

Cigar makers roll tobacco from Central America and the Dominican Republic in San Diego's original cigar factory. Aficionados can select from a variety of cigars.

9 United Nations International Gift Shop
MAP L2 ■ 2171 Pan American Plaza ■ (619) 233-5044

Toys, instruments, jewelry, books, crafts, and ethnic clothing are among the temptations at this colorful store.

10 Dolcetti Boutique
MAP K5 ■ 635 5th Ave ■ (619) 501-1559

One of the preferred stops for special occasion pieces. There's also a regularly updated sales rack, plus a good selection of jewelry, accessories, and men's clothing.

Museum Shops

Jewelry at the Museum of Art shop

1 San Diego Museum of Art

Exhibit-led art books, stationery, jewelry, purses, flower pressing kits, and Tibetan chests are for sale. The children's section offers educational toys and gifts (see p22).

2 Mingei International Museum

This store is filled with ethnic clothes, Chinese brushes, Russian dolls, Indian chiming bells, and a good selection of alebrijes (see p22).

3 San Diego Museum of Man

Crafts from around Latin America include Peruvian gourds, Mexican folk art, and three-legged Chilean good luck pigs. There is also a wide range of Native American crafts such as silver jewelry (see p22).

4 Museum of Contemporary Art

Check out the select merchandise that relates to the museum's special exhibitions. The latest art books and handcrafted jewelry are always on offer (see p79).

5 San Diego Art Institute Shop

MAP L1 ■ House of Charm, Balboa Pk
Juried art shows present the work of local artists, whose works often go on sale after being exhibited. This small shop features glass sculptures, porcelain objets d'art, hand-painted cushions, and jewelry.

6 Maritime Museum of San Diego

Gratify your nautical gift needs with a variety of model ships, T-shirts, posters, and prints inscribed with an image of the Star of India (see p47).

7 Reuben H. Fleet Science Center

Science toys, videos, puzzles, and hands-on games here are very popular with the kids (see p59).

8 San Diego Chinese Historical Museum

Chinese calligraphy sets, tea sets, snuff bottles, and chops – a type of carved stamp used to sign one's name – are on sale here (see p46).

Store at Museum of Photographic Arts

9 Museum of Photographic Arts

Exhibition catalogs, prints, note cards, and calendars represent the world's finest photographic artists, both past and present. A wide range of books is also available (see p22).

10 San Diego History Center

If you're interested in San Diego's past, including haunted locations and biographies, this museum offers one of the best collections of local history books (see p22).

See map on pp76–7 ←

Cruising the Bay

Aerial view of Coronado Bridge

① Coronado Bridge
This bridge links Coronado to San Diego. Its gradual incline and curve allow cars to maintain speed. It is high enough for aircraft carriers to pass beneath at high tide *(see p28)*.

② SPAWAR
MAP B5

This Navy marine mammal facility trains bottlenose dolphins, with their biological sonar, to locate sea mines.

③ Naval Base San Diego
MAP D6

This base provides shore support and living quarters for more than 50 naval ships of the Pacific Fleet, and is one of only two major fleet support installations in the country.

④ Naval Air Station North Island
MAP B5

Several aircraft carriers tie up here. You can often see high-tech aircraft, submarines, and destroyers.

⑤ Local Marine Wildlife
Seals and sea lions are bay residents. The East Pacific green sea turtle and the California least tern have protected foraging habitats.

⑥ Naval Amphibious Base
Home to the Navy SEALS and the Navy Parachute Team, the facility has served as a training base since 1943. It is responsible for training and maintenance of the ships of the Pacific Fleet *(see p28)*.

⑦ Cabrillo National Monument
Dedicated to the European discovery of San Diego and Alta California, this monument draws over one million people a year. The statue of Cabrillo is a replica of an original that could not withstand the wind and salt air *(see p30)*.

⑧ NASSCO Shipyard
MAP D6

The National Steel and Shipbuilding Company designs and builds US Navy auxiliary ships, commercial tankers, and container ships. It is one of the largest shipyards in the US.

⑨ Museum Vessels of the Embarcadero
The sailing ship *Star of India* dates back to 1863; *Berkeley* used to carry passengers in the Bay Area; and the USS *Midway* features in the USS Midway Museum *(see pp14–17)*.

The *Star of India* on the Embarcadero

⑩ Cruise Ship Terminal
MAP G4

San Diego boasts the fastest-growing cruise ship port on the west coast, with 180 ships docking at the B Street Pier throughout the year. Cruises leave for excursions to the Mexican Riviera, Hawaii, Canada, the Panama Canal, and the South Pacific.

Places to Eat

PRICE CATEGORIES
Price categories include a three-course meal for one, half a bottle of wine, and all unavoidable extra charges including tax.
....
$ under $40 $$ $40–$80 $$$ over $80

1 Oceanaire Seafood Room
MAP J5 ▪ 400 J St ▪ (619) 858-2277 ▪ $$

The creative menu here features seafood from around the world. The oysters and crab cakes are legendary.

2 Kansas City Barbeque
MAP H5 ▪ 600 W. Harbor Drive ▪ (619) 231-9680 ▪ $

This busy eatery shot to fame as a setting in the iconic film *Top Gun*. It serves big plates of barbecue favorites with traditional sides.

3 The Grant Grill
MAP J4 ▪ US Grant Hotel, 326 Broadway ▪ (619) 744-2077 ▪ $$

With a club-like ambience, The Grant Grill offers contemporary California cuisine. Try the famous mock turtle soup with chervil and sherry.

4 Top of the Market
MAP G5 ▪ 750 N. Harbor Dr ▪ (619) 232-3474 ▪ $$$

Chichi seafood restaurant with fabulous views. Come here for a window seat, a calm atmosphere, and seafood prepared with panache.

5 Karl Strauss' Brewing Company
MAP H4 ▪ 1157 Columbia St ▪ (619) 234-2739 ▪ $

Try the outstanding burgers, blackened salmon, or baby back ribs. Wash it all down with one of the hand-crafted house brews on offer.

6 Downtown Fish Joint
MAP J4 ▪ 407 C St ▪ (619) 239-3506 ▪ Closed Sun ▪ $

Food here is fun, fresh, filling, and cheap: try the salmon and chips (which are actually waffle fries). Service is fast, business is brisk, and the atmosphere is casual.

7 Lou & Mickey's
MAP J6 ▪ 224 5th Ave ▪ (619) 237-4900 ▪ $$$

Delectable steaks, fresh seafood, and pasta dishes are served at booths, tables, or on a shaded patio.

Patio area at Lou & Mickey's

8 Tender Greens
MAP J4 ▪ 110 W. Broadway ▪ (619) 795-2353 ▪ $

There's something for everyone here – from fried chicken and hearty salads, to vegan options and soups.

9 St. Tropez Bakery & Bistro
MAP H4 ▪ 600 W. Broadway/130 America Plaza ▪ (619) 234-2560 ▪ $

Feast on stuffed croissants, crêpes, and well-prepared salads. Save room for utterly delicious pastries. A little wine bar is also attached.

10 Indigo Grill
MAP H3 ▪ 1536 India St ▪ (619) 234-6802 ▪ $$

This Little Italy restaurant serves food with a modern Latin kick. Try the tacos with jalapeno tartare sauce or spicy honey aioli.

See map on pp76–7

🔟 Old Town, Uptown, and Mission Valley

This long stretch follows the San Diego River from the Mission San Diego de Alcalá to Old Town. Over 200 years ago, the Kumeyaay tribe lived in small settlements in the valley, unaware that strangers from the other side of the earth would change their lives forever. Both Spanish soldiers and Franciscan padres had glory here, as well as San Diego's pioneer families. The valley itself holds little interest beyond masses of chain motels and shopping centers intersected by a freeway; however, on the bluffs above, you'll find eclectic neighborhoods overflowing with charm, brilliant architecture, and chic restaurants. Tolerance and diversity creates a progressive, Bohemian air, while rising real estate prices have turned simple bungalow homes into showpieces. And San Diego's birthplace is always close by.

Mormon Battalion Memorial

AREA MAP OF OLD TOWN, UPTOWN, AND MISSION VALLEY

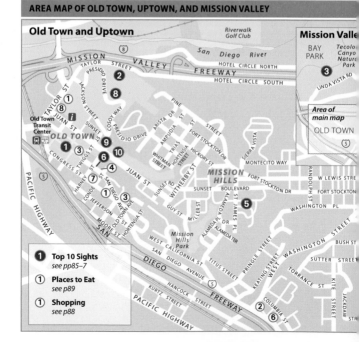

1 Top 10 Sights
see pp85–7

1 Places to Eat
see p89

1 Shopping
see p88

① Old Town State Historic Park

San Diego's first commercial settlement has been either preserved or re-created in this pedestrian-only park. Much of the town was destroyed in a fire in 1872, prompting the development of a new town center closer to the water, but several original structures remain. You can wander into any of Old Town's houses and find museums or concession shops inside (see pp26–7).

② Junípero Serra Museum
MAP P4 ▪ 2727 Presidio Dr ▪ (619) 232-6203 ▪ Open Jun–Sep 4: 10am–5pm Tue–Sun; Sep 5–May: 10am–5pm Sat & Sun ▪ Adm ▪ www.sandiegohistory.org

Constructed in 1929 to a design by William Templeton Johnson, the museum building is in keeping with the city's Spanish-Colonial heritage. Its white stucco arches, narrow passages, red-tile roof, and stately tower pay tribute to the first mission, which stood near this site. Artifacts from ongoing archeological excavations, ceramics made by Kumeyaay Indians, clothing, furniture, and a cannon help illustrate the meager life people led. Climb the tower to compare today's view with that of 1929.

③ University of San Diego
MAP C4 ▪ 5998 Alcalá Park ▪ (619) 260-4600

Grand Spanish Renaissance buildings distinguish this independent Catholic university, its design inspired by the university in the Spanish town of Alcalá de Henares. Of exceptional note is the Founders Chapel with its white marble altar, gold-leaf decoration, 14 stained-glass nave windows, and marble floor.

University of San Diego

④ Mission Basilica San Diego de Alcalá

A peaceful enclave among the nondescript strip malls of Mission Valley, the mission's original spirit still lingers in the church and its lovely gardens. The first of California's 21 missions was moved to this permanent site a few years after its founding. Over the years, the structure was rebuilt to suit the needs of the time. Its famous façade and bell tower have inspired architects to copy the "Mission Style" throughout San Diego (see pp32–3).

5 Mission Hills
MAP Q5 ▪ Mission Hills
Nursery: 1525 Fort Stockton Dr

One of San Diego's most charming and romantic neighborhoods is in the hills overlooking Old Town and San Diego Bay. Tree-lined streets run past architectural jewels built in various styles. Dating from the early 1900s, homes had to cost at least $3,500, and could not keep any male farm animals. Only those of Caucasian descent could hold property. Kate Sessions' 1910 nursery *(see p23)* can still be visited here.

Interior of haunted Whaley House

6 Whaley House Museum
MAP P5 ▪ 2482 San Diego Ave ▪ (619) 297-7511 ▪ Open 10am–4:30pm Sun–Tue, 10am–9:30pm Thu–Sat; late May–early Sep: 10am–9:30pm daily ▪ Adm ▪ whaleyhouse.org

California's first two-story brick structure also served as San Diego's first courthouse, county seat, and home to Thomas Whaley, who built it in 1856 over a graveyard and site of a former gallows. The US Commerce Department declared the house officially haunted in the 1960s.

7 Hillcrest
MAP C4

Considered San Diego's first suburb in the 1920s, Hillcrest slowly developed into a residential area, offering a quiet alternative to the bustle of downtown. A trolley stop opened the neighborhood up to thriving businesses, restaurants, and theaters; in the 1940s, merchants

APOLINARIA LORENZANA

In 1800, Apolinaria Lorenzana and 20 orphans arrived from Mexico to be distributed to respectable presidio families. She taught herself to write by copying every written thing she found. She spent her life caring for the mission padres, teaching children and women church doctrine, and tending the sick. Nicknamed La Beata, she was one of the few women to receive a land grant.

proudly erected a sign that spanned University Boulevard, proclaiming "Hillcrest" to the world. But fortunes changed, neglect followed, and the sign came down. In the 1970s, the gay and lesbian community took up the revitalization challenge and transformed the community into a hip destination with great restaurants, nightlife, and avant-garde shops. And now the sign is back – in neon.

8 Presidio Park
MAP P5

Kumeyaay Indians once used this hillside for sacred ceremonies. Site of the original Spanish presidio and mission settlement, a lovely park is all that's left of San Diego's beginnings. The park contains the Junípero Serra Museum *(see p85)* and the remaining earthen walls of Fort Stockton, a fortress that changed hands several times during the Mexican-American War, marked by bronze monuments, a flagpole, and a cannon. The 28-ft (8.5-m)

Serra Cross, constructed from mission tiles, honors founder Saint Junípero Serra (see p32).

9 Mormon Battalion Memorial Visitor's Center

MAP P5 ∎ 2510 Juan St ∎ (619) 298-3317 ∎ Open 9am–9pm daily

In July 1846, 500 men, 32 women, and 51 children set out from Council Bluffs, Iowa, on what would be considered one of the longest military marches in history. Six months and 2,000 miles (3,218 km) later, they reached San Diego to support the American military garrison in the Mexican-American War. At the Visitor's Center, a volunteer from the Church of Latter-Day Saints discusses the march and Mormon contributions to the area.

10 Heritage Park

MAP P5 ∎ 2454 Heritage Park Row ∎ (619) 819-6009 ∎ Open 9am–5pm daily

Downtown's rapid expansion after World War II almost destroyed several Victorian heritage houses and San Diego's first synagogue. The Save Our Heritage Organization rescued and moved these architectural treasures to this specially created park. Of notable interest is the Sherman Gilbert House, once home to art and music patrons Bess and Gertrude Gilbert, who hosted luminaries such as Artur Rubinstein, Anna Pavlova, and the Trapp Family Singers.

Houses in Heritage Park

A WALK AROUND OLD TOWN, HERITAGE PARK, AND PRESIDIO PARK

▶ MORNING

Begin at the **Old Town Transit Center**. Cross the street and follow the path into **Old Town State Historic Park**. Just to the left is the **Interpretive Center**, where you can pick up a map. Walk along the right side of the Plaza and peek into the Bailey & McGuire Pottery Shop. Follow the signs to **La Casa de Machado y Stewart** (see p27) and the **Mason Street School** (see p26). Back at the Plaza, visit **La Casa de Estudillo** (see p26) for the best insight into an upper-class home of early California. From the Plaza's southwest corner, continue out of the State Park. Walk along San Diego Avenue, where you'll find souvenir shops, galleries, and restaurants. Try the **Old Town Mexican Café** (see p89) for lunch.

AFTERNOON

Cross the street at Conde and backtrack up San Diego Avenue to visit the haunted **Whaley House**. Turn right on Harney Street and walk uphill to **Heritage Park**. Backtrack one block to the **Mormon Battalion Visitor's Center**. Turn right on Juan Street and walk to Mason. You'll see a sign indicating "The Old Presidio Historic Trail." Turn right on Mason, follow the golf course to Jackson, and look for the footpath across the street. You'll parallel Jackson to the left and wind uphill to **Presidio Park**. Across the grass are the ruins of the original presidio, the **Serra Cross**, and the **Junípero Serra Museum**.

See map on pp84–5 ←

Shopping

1 Bazaar del Mundo
MAP N5 = 4133 Taylor St
= (619) 296-3161

In a lushly landscaped plaza, quality shops offer Mexican tableware, folk art, Guatemalan textiles, and books.

2 Gioia's Room
MAP C4 = 3739 6th Ave = (619) 269–2303

An interesting boutique that offers accessories and vintage women's clothing with free alterations.

3 Old Town Market
MAP N5 = 4010 Twiggs St
= (619) 260-1078

This festive market offers entertainment and local artisans. The shops sell colorful Mexican goods, such as Day of the Dead folk art, as well as jewelry and gifts.

Mexican crucifixes, Old Town Market

4 Four Winds Trading Company
MAP P5 = 2448-B San Diego Ave
= (619) 692-0466

This Old Town store specializes in authentic Indian pottery, weavings, jewelry, dreamcatchers, and paintings of Native American themes.

5 Record City
MAP C4 = 3757 6th Ave = (619) 291-5313

There's nothing quite like vinyl, and the crates here are stocked with rock and 1980s and 1990s alternative music. Used CDs are also on sale.

6 5th Avenue Books
MAP C4 = 3838 5th Ave = (619) 291-4660

The library-like shelves in this independent shop feature science-fiction, fantasy, new-age, feminist, poetry, and art books, as well as contemporary and classic fiction.

7 Creative Crossroads
MAP C4 = 502 University Ave
= (800) 685-2513

Local artisans show and sell their wares in this marketplace near the corner of University and Fifth. Purchase jewelry, greeting cards, art, gifts, and Gay Pride apparel.

8 Bluestocking Books
MAP C4 = 3817 5th Ave = (619) 296-1424

This independent store offers new and used books on a wide range of subjects. The search service aims to locate rare and vintage items.

9 Whole Foods
MAP C4 = 711 University Ave
= (619) 294-2800

With an emphasis on fresh organic food, you'll find flavorful produce, a great assortment of imported goods, and a deli that specializes in healthy takeout.

10 Adams Avenue & Park Boulevard Antique Row
Adams Ave: MAP D4 = Park Blvd:
MAP D4

Still untouched by San Diego's urban renewal boom, antique stores, second-hand book and record shops, and retro-clothing boutiques are sprinkled along these streets in east Hillcrest and Normal Heights.

Places to Eat

1 Jack and Giulio's Italian Restaurant
MAP P5 ▪ 2391 San Diego Ave ▪ (619) 294-2074 ▪ $$

Classics like Caprese salad, scampi, and tiramisu are served in a romantic and intimate space – a welcome respite from the crowds in Old Town.

Thai dishes are served up at Saffron

2 Saffron
MAP C4 ▪ 3731 India St ▪ (619) 574-7737 ▪ $

Parking is tricky, but crowds come here for wondrously flavorful Thai cuisine. Takeout is also available.

3 El Agave Tequileria
MAP P6 ▪ 2304 San Diego Ave ▪ (619) 220-0692 ▪ $$

Utter culinary magic awaits within one of the first tequilarias in San Diego. Classic Mexican food with modern touches (see p64).

4 Crest Café
MAP C4 ▪ 425 Robinson Ave ▪ (619) 295-2510 ▪ $

Locals love this upscale diner, serving fresh soups, salads, and big burgers.

Dessert at Crest Café

5 Arrivederci Ristorante
MAP C4 ▪ 3845 4th Ave ▪ (619) 299-6282 ▪ $$

Service at this cozy spot is friendly, prices are reasonable, and the pasta dishes are some of the best in town.

PRICE CATEGORIES
Price categories include a three-course meal for one, half a bottle of wine, and all unavoidable extra charges including tax.

$ under $40 $$ $40–$80 $$$ over $80

6 Blue Water Seafood Market & Grill
MAP C4 ▪ 3667 India St ▪ (619) 497-0914 ▪ $

A fabulous selection of seafood is on offer at this friendly seafood market. Try the fish tacos, seafood cocktails, or chowders.

7 Old Town Mexican Café & Cantina
MAP P5 ▪ 2489 San Diego Ave ▪ (619) 297-4330 ▪ $$

Watch the famous "Tortilla Ladies of Old Town." People line up to try the café's grilled pork *carnitas* and *chilaquiles*, a tortilla strip casserole.

8 Casa Guadalajara
MAP N5 ▪ 4105 Taylor St ▪ (619) 295-5111 ▪ $$

This festive restaurant is a grand celebration of Mexican specialties and premium margaritas, along with folk art, fountains, and mariachis.

9 Brooklyn Girl Eatery
MAP C4 ▪ 4033 Goldfinch St ▪ (619) 296-4600 ▪ $$

Savor seasonal menus with locally sourced products. Try the bacon-wrapped Vietnamese meatballs.

10 San Diego Chicken Pie Shop
MAP D4 ▪ 2633 El Cajon, North Park ▪ (619) 295-0156 ▪ No credit cards ▪ $

Seniors and budget-eaters love the hearty food here: think tasty chicken pies accompanied by mashed potatoes and gravy.

See map on pp84–5

TOP 10 Ocean Beach, Coronado, and the South

South of San Diego to the Mexican border, cultures blend in several communities. Many Mexicans live, work, and send their children to schools in these border areas; others cross into the US for shopping. While many Americans used to enjoy reciprocal pleasures in Mexico, sadly drug-cartel violence has spilled into Tijuana and other tourist zones. There are good experiences to be had on the US side, particularly in Chula Vista.

Point Loma

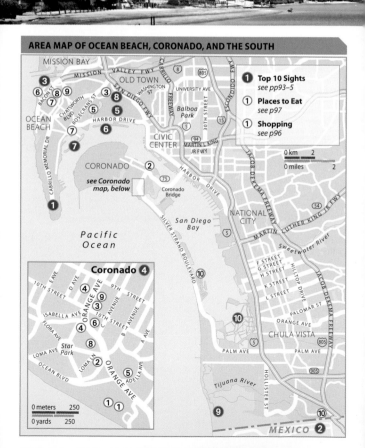

AREA MAP OF OCEAN BEACH, CORONADO, AND THE SOUTH

❶ Top 10 Sights
see pp93–5

❶ Places to Eat
see p97

❶ Shopping
see p96

0 km   2
0 miles   2

Previous pages The Botanical Building and the Lily Pond in Balboa Park

1 Point Loma

Over one million people a year visit the Cabrillo National Monument at Point Loma. The views are mesmerizing, and the peninsula ends at the meeting point of the Pacific Ocean and San Diego Bay. Half the peninsula is occupied by the military, preventing overdevelopment. Spend time at Sunset Cliffs Park and perhaps spot a whale (see pp30–31).

2 Tijuana

During the days of Prohibition, Tijuana, Mexico, used to be the destination of choice for the Hollywood elite and their followers, and for alcohol and gambling. The palatial, Moorish-designed Agua Caliente Casino & Spa was so popular that it boasted its own landing airstrip for the private planes of the wealthy. Fortunes fell when Mexico declared casino gambling illegal in 1935, and the city later reinvented itself as a family-oriented tourist destination. In recent years, however, drug cartel violence has escalated, and visitors should be diligent and heed all published government warnings.

3 Ocean Beach

Unconventional and laid back, OB, as it's locally known, has a somewhat hippie-like feel. On main thoroughfare Newport Avenue, you can still find a few original shops. But OB is mainly about the beach: on any day of the year, surfers are waiting for the next swell; volleyball players are spiking balls over the net; and dogs are running freely on Dog Beach (see p53).

The famous Hotel del Coronado

4 Coronado

In the 1880s, two wealthy businessmen, Elisha Babcock, Jr. and Hampton Story, purchased Coronado and set out to build a town. They sold lots, laid streets, and constructed the landmark Hotel del Coronado (see p28). John D. Spreckels (see p43) soon bought them out and turned Coronado into a haven for old-money gentry. The military permanently took over much of the peninsula during World War I. The old mansions, resorts, and military base exist harmoniously and give Coronado its unique identity (see pp28–9).

5 San Diego International Airport

MAP G2

No matter where you are in San Diego, look up and you'll see a jet soaring dramatically past the downtown high-rises on its final approach to Lindbergh Field (see p44). One hundred years ago, this area was a muddy wasteland that proved to be an ideal spot for budding inventors and pilots to try out their latest machines. In 1927, Ryan Aviation designed, produced, and tested on the beach the *Spirit of St. Louis*, the historic plane that Charles Lindbergh piloted solo across the Atlantic.

Surfer at Ocean Beach

Boats moored in the marina at Harbor Island

6 Harbor Island
MAP C5

Created from 3.5 million tons of mud from the bottom of San Diego Bay, this recreational island is a peninsula that extends into the bay south from the airport. Hotels, restaurants, and marinas offer gorgeous views across the bay of downtown, Point Loma, and Coronado. Facing the island is Spanish Landing Park, which commemorates the 1769 meeting of the sea and land expeditions of Gaspar de Portolá and Junípero Serra (see p42), which permanently brought the Spanish to California.

Shoreline Park on Shelter Island

7 Shelter Island
MAP B5

Not really an island but a peninsula that juts out into San Diego Bay from Point Loma, this is home to pleasure boats and a park along its length. In the 1950s, the city dredged millions of tons of sand and mud from the bay onto a sandbar to create land for marinas and hotels. A number of hotels still have hints of Polynesian themes, a popular style at the time. The San Diego Yacht Club here is the three-time host of the prestigious America's Cup sailing race.

8 Marine Corps Recruit Depot
MAP B5 ■ 1600 Henderson Ave ■ (619) 524-6719 ■ Open 8am–4pm Mon–Sat (photo ID for Depot; proof of insurance if driving)

Listed on the National Register of Historic Places, the quaint Spanish-Colonial buildings were designed by Bertram Goodhue, architect of several buildings for the Panama-California Exposition in Balboa Park (see pp18–19). The Command Museum displays the history of the

---

TENT CITY

When John D. Spreckels acquired the Hotel del Coronado in 1890, he felt the beauty of the area should be available to everyone. He built "Tent City," a makeshift town that catered to the less-well-to-do. Arriving by rail and car, families paid $4.50 a week to live in tents equipped with beds, dressers, and flush toilets. Amenities included carnival booths, Japanese gardens, a library, and children's bull fights. At its peak, the town held 10,000 visitors. The tents came down by 1939, when they could no longer compete with the rising popularity of the roadside motel.

Marine Corps in Southern California and the wars in which they fought. Exhibits include photos, training films, and a World War II ambulance.

9 Border Field State Park

As the endangered Western snowy plover seeks a place to lay her eggs, the green-and-white vehicles of the US Border Patrol swoop down hillsides, lights blazing, in search of an illegal immigrant. An enormous, rusty, corrugated metal fence, which separates the US and Mexico, slices through the park before plunging into the sea. This southern part of the Tijuana River National Estuarine Research Reserve (see p51) attracts nature lovers who come to hike, ride horses, picnic on the beach, and bird-watch. On the Mexican side of the fence is a lively Mexican community and bullring (see p45).

Owl, Living Coast Discovery Center

10 Living Coast Discovery Center

MAP E3 ■ 1000 Gunpowder Point, Chula Vista ■ (619) 409-5900 ■ Open 9am–5pm daily ■ Adm

The center is in the Sweetwater Marsh National Wildlife Refuge, one of the few accessible salt marshes left on the Pacific Coast. Rent some binoculars and climb to an observation deck to see how many of the 200 bird species in the refuge you can spot. Or you can also take a self-guided tour along interpretative trails. Children will enjoy petting bat rays and leopard sharks. The parking lot is located near the Baysite/E Street Trolley Station; a free shuttle will take you to the center.

A BIKE RIDE AROUND CORONADO

MORNING

Begin at **Bikes & Beyond** (see p54) at the **Ferry Landing Market Place**. Walk to the sidewalk facing the harbor and enjoy the city view. Pedestrians and joggers also use this sidewalk, so proceed cautiously. Around the corner, you'll face the **Coronado Bridge** (see p28); the bougainvillea-covered walls on the right mark the **Marriott Resort** (see p116). Information boards on the way depict harbor wildlife and a map indicates the various navy yards. Under the bridge, the path turns away from the water. At the street, bear left and cross over. There is no protected bike path, but traffic is light on **Glorietta Blvd**.

At the marina, the road will fork; take the lower road to the left. Turn right at the stop-light and get off your bike; bike riding is forbidden on Orange Avenue. At 1025 Orange Avenue, **Moo Time Creamery** serves delicious home-made ice cream and smoothies. Walk your bike back to the **Hotel del Coronado** (see p28) and check out the shops on its lower level (see p96). Leaving the hotel, bear left to Ocean Avenue; the Pacific Ocean is on the left and several mansions, built in the 1900s–1920s, are on the right. Turn right on Alameda and ride through a typical Coronado neighborhood with Spanish-style houses and bungalows. At 4th, cross the street and walk one block; the **Naval Air Station** will be on your left. Turn right on 1st. It's a straight stretch back to the Market Place.

See map on p92

Shopping

① Shops at the Hotel del Coronado

You'll find some of the best shopping in Coronado among these extensive shops in the hotel, including women's upscale casual wear, sunglasses, toys, jewelry, and the books of L. Frank Baum (see p28).

Ferry Landing Marketplace

② Ferry Landing Marketplace
MAP C6

Next to the Coronado Ferry dock (see p29), this place offers an eclectic selection of souvenirs, clothing, and galleries. A great farmers' market sets up on Tuesday afternoons.

③ Bookstar/Loma Theatre
MAP B4 ■ 3150 Rosecrans Place ■ (619) 225-0465

Barnes & Noble's branded store Bookstar is set in the vintage Loma Theatre, with its original façade, and makes for a special experience.

④ Coronado Museum of History and Art Store

Head to this museum store for historic photos, posters, and books, as well as a fun selection of *Wizard of Oz*-themed gifts – author L. Frank Baum lived in Coronado (see pp28–9).

⑤ Liberty Station
MAP B5 ■ 2640 Historic Decatur ■ (619) 573-9300

The Spanish Colonial-Revival buildings of the former Naval Training Center promote an elegant shopping experience. You'll find grocers, wine shops, bakeries, chocolatiers, ethnic jewelry, and more.

⑥ Bay Books
MAP C6 ■ 1029 Orange Ave, Coronado ■ (619) 435-0070

This independent bookstore has helpful staff, an ample selection of books of local interest and international papers and magazines.

⑦ Newport Avenue
MAP B4 ■ Ocean Beach

The main drag through Ocean Beach is chock full of antique shops. Some doorways front malls with dozens of shops inside. Finds range from 1950s retro pieces to Victorian and Asian antiques.

⑧ Ocean Beach People's Organic Food Market
MAP B4 ■ 4765 Voltaire St ■ (619) 224-1387

This co-op market has been selling organic, minimally processed natural foods since 1971. For food to go, try the upstairs vegan deli. Non-members are welcome but will be charged a small percentage more.

⑨ Blue Jeans and Bikinis
MAP C6 ■ 971 Orange Ave, Coronado ■ (619) 319-5858

The trendiest blue jeans, along with a wide selection of bikinis, boots, and accessories, are all part of the changing inventory here.

⑩ Las Americas Premium Outlets
MAP E3 ■ San Ysidro

Within walking distance of the border with Mexico, you can stop by this immense 560,000-sq-ft (52,000-sq-m) outlet center (see pp114–5).

Places to Eat

1 1500 Ocean
MAP C6 ▪ Hotel del Coronado, 1500 Orange Ave ▪ (619) 435-6611 ▪ $$$

The atmosphere here is light, as is the cuisine. There is a good choice of wines from Southern California's finest vineyards.

2 Chez Loma
MAP C6 ▪ 1132 Loma Ave, Coronado ▪ (619) 435-0661 ▪ Closed Mon ▪ Limited dis. access ▪ $$

The luscious French cuisine will put you in heaven. Diners can get great-value meals in the early-bird special.

3 Clayton's Coffee Shop
MAP C6 ▪ 979 Orange Ave ▪ (619) 435-5425 ▪ No dis. access ▪ No credit cards ▪ $

Come here for home-style cooking. A quarter buys three jukebox plays.

4 Primavera Ristorante
MAP C6 ▪ 932 Orange Ave, Coronado ▪ (619) 435-0454 ▪ $$$

Legendary northern Italian cuisine is served here in an intimate setting. The tiramisu is exceptional.

5 Miguel's Cocina
MAP C6 ▪ 1351 Orange Ave, Coronado ▪ (619) 437-4237 ▪ $$

Colorfully dressed waitresses serve up enormous plates and lethal margaritas. The enchiladas, tacos, and burritos are delicious.

Outdoor patio at Miguel's Cocina

PRICE CATEGORIES

Price categories include a three-course meal for one, half a bottle of wine, and all unavoidable extra charges including tax.

$ under $40 $$ $40–$80 $$$ over $80

6 Hodad's
MAP A4 ▪ 5010 Newport Ave ▪ (619) 224-4623 ▪ $

Soak up the "junkyard Gothic" ambience at this beach café devoted to burgers, brews, and surf.

7 Point Loma Seafoods
MAP B5 ▪ 2805 Emerson St ▪ (619) 223-1109 ▪ $

Order the freshest seafood in San Diego. Salads and sushi are popular.

8 Café 1134
MAP C6 ▪ 1134 Orange Ave, Coronado ▪ (619) 437-1134 ▪ $

This café with a patio offers a selection of sandwiches, wraps, and panini. Breakfast is served all day.

9 Peace Pies
MAP B4 ▪ 4230 Voltaire St ▪ (619) 223-2880 ▪ $

Pick up picnic fare or eat in the small dining area or on the outdoor patio. All choices are vegan and gluten free.

10 Mistral
MAP E2 ▪ Loews Coronado Bay Resort, 4000 Coronado Bay Rd ▪ (619) 424-4000 ▪ $$

Enjoy California-Mediterranean cuisine with views across the bay.

TOP 10 Northern San Diego

San Diego's explosive growth has been concentrated in North County, formerly an area of wide-open spaces. Prosperous high-tech, biotech, commercial, and financial businesses have relocated here and play a major role in the city's development. Over one million people live in communities with distinct identities, from the high-end rural estates of Rancho Santa Fe to the more modest housing of Marine Corps families in Oceanside. Travel through fabled beach resorts into laid-back surfer towns and active Camp Pendleton Marine Base, or head east from Oceanside past flower farms and avocado groves, filled with blooms and fruit.

Fountain in the San Diego Botanic Garden

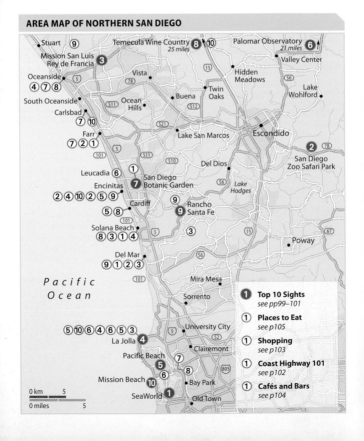

AREA MAP OF NORTHERN SAN DIEGO

1	**Top 10 Sights** see pp99–101
①	**Places to Eat** see p105
①	**Shopping** see p103
①	**Coast Highway 101** see p102
①	**Cafés and Bars** see p104

0 km   5
0 miles   5

1 SeaWorld

MAP B4 ■ 500 Sea World Dr, Mission Bay ■ (619) 226-3901 ■ Open daily ■ Adm (special prices online) ■ www.seaworld.com/sandiego

Opened in 1964, SeaWorld covers 150 acres (60 ha) of Mission Bay and allows visitors to see many ocean creatures up close. Its family-oriented thrill rides can compete with those of most adventure parks. It also has a rehabilitation program for stranded marine animals. However, less positive aspects of SeaWorld have come to light since the release of the 2013 documentary *Blackfish*. The park has come under strong criticism, seeing a downturn in public opinion and visitors.

2 San Diego Zoo Safari Park

MAP E2 ■ 15500 San Pasqual Valley Rd, Escondido ■ (760) 747-8702 ■ Open 9am–5pm daily (mid-Jun–mid-Sep & mid- to end Dec: to 9pm) ■ Adm

Many people prefer the Zoo Safari Park to its sister zoo in Balboa Park *(see pp20–21)*. By monorail, zipline, or a range of safaris, experience African and Asian animals roaming freely in enormous enclosures. Don't miss the Tull Family Tiger Trail, which takes you up close to Sumatran tigers. A successful breeding program works with more than 165 endangered species, including rhinos and lions.

3 Mission San Luis Rey de Francia

MAP D1 ■ 4050 Mission Ave, Oceanside ■ (760) 757-3651 (ext. 117) ■ Open 9am–5pm Mon–Fri, 10am–5pm Sat & Sun ■ Adm ■ www.sanluisrey.org

Named after canonized French king Louis IX, this mission was the last established in Southern California. Relations between the missionaries and the indigenous population were so successful that when Father Peyri was ordered by the Mexican government to return to Spain in 1832, the Native Americans followed him to San Diego Harbor. Today's restored mission has displays on life and artifacts of the mission era and also offers popular retreats.

Mission San Luis Rey de Francia

4 La Jolla

Surrounded on three sides by ocean bluffs and beaches boasting spectacular views, this gorgeous enclave is noted for upscale shops, boutiques, and fine-dining restaurants. Often cited as having the most expensive properties in the country, it is also home to several prestigious educational and research facilities *(see p100)*. Torrey Pines offers a number of hiking trails and the famous Torrey Pines Golf Course *(see p37)*.

La Jolla cove

5 Pacific Beach
MAP A3

Residents here enjoy an endless summer climate and easy-going lifestyle. Life revolves around Garnet Avenue's nightclubs, cafés, late-night restaurants, and shops. The street ends at the 1927 Crystal Pier, a great spot to see surfers, or spend a night in a tiny cottage. Come early to claim a fire ring on the beach and cook up some marshmallows, or cycle the boardwalk to Mission Beach *(see p53)*.

Hale Telescope, Palomar Observatory

6 Palomar Observatory
MAP E1 ▪ 35899 Canfield Road, Palomar Mountain ▪ (760) 742-2119 ▪ Open 9am–3pm daily (until 4pm Apr–Oct)

Atop one of North County's highest mountains, the dome of the observatory has an otherworldly look. Part of the California Institute of Technology, Palomar is home to the 200-in (508-cm) Hale Telescope, the largest optical instrument of its kind when installed in 1947. Its moving parts weigh 530 tons, the mirror 14.5 tons. Thanks to computer technology, no one "looks" through the telescope anymore. Self-guided tours offer a look at the telescope itself.

BRAIN POWER

Beneath San Diego's "fun in the sun" image is one of the country's most educated populations. With one of the nation's highest incidences of PhDs per capita, 30 percent of residents hold college degrees, and 20 percent of adults are in higher education. La Jolla boasts some of the most prestigious research facilities: the Salk Institute, Scripps Research Institute, Scripps Institution of Oceanography, and UC San Diego.

7 San Diego Botanic Garden
MAP D2 ▪ 230 Quail Gardens Drive, Encinitas ▪ (760) 436-3036 ▪ Open 9am–5pm daily (exc. Christmas Day) ▪ Adm

This is a treasure-packed expanse of nearly two dozen gardens on well-marked pathways, with viewpoints, sculpture exhibits, garden shops, and plenty of opportunities for bird-watching. Dedicated areas display Australian, African, Mexican, and Central American gardens; succulents and dragon trees; and the country's largest bamboo collection. There's also a Native Plants and Native People trail.

8 Temecula Wine Country
MAP E1 ▪ Thornton Winery: 32575 Rancho California Rd; (951) 699-0099 ▪ Callaway Vineyard & Winery: 32720 Rancho California Rd; (951) 676-4001

During the mission days, Franciscan friars recognized that San Diego's soil and climate were ideal for planting grape vines. However, it wasn't until the 1960s that wine was first produced commercially. Now over two dozen wineries stretch across rolling hills studded with oak trees, most of them along Rancho

California Road. Wineries offer tastings for a small fee, and many of them operate restaurants and delis. Two of the most popular wineries in the area are Thornton Winery and Callaway Vineyard & Winery.

9 Rancho Santa Fe

This well-kept secret enclave, about 5 miles (8 km) east of the coast, harbors exquisite estates for the wealthy. Home to around 3,000 residents, in 1989, The Covenant of Rancho Santa Fe was designated a California Historical Landmark as a historic planned community. Responsibility for this honor rests with architect Lillian Rice, who designed it in 1921. It is a lovely place to explore and dine in.

Luxurious living in Rancho Santa Fe

10 Mission Beach
MAP A4

The California beach scene struts in full glory along a narrow strip of land filled with vacation rentals and beachwear shops (see p53). Skaters, cyclists, and joggers whiz along the Strand, while surfers and sun worshipers pack the sand. Sometimes the streets become so crowded on the Fourth of July weekend that the police have to shut the area down. A block away, Belmont Park (see p59) is an old-fashioned fun zone with a vintage roller coaster.

Temecula Wine Country

A MORNING IN LA JOLLA

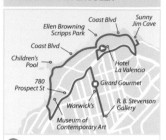

▶ MORNING

Begin by looking out the front door of the landmark **La Valencia Hotel** (see p118). Turn left onto Prospect Street and walk past restaurants and art galleries. Before you reach Coast Boulevard, a stairway to the left leads to the **Sunny Jim Cave**, a fascinating, ocean-carved cave, named by L. Frank Baum (see p43). To the left of the entrance, a platform overlooks the caves. Continue along Coast Boulevard, admiring views of Torrey Pines and Scripps Pier. Pass through **Ellen Browning Scripps Park** (see p51). Beyond the end of the park is **Children's Pool** (see p58). Check out the seals and sea lions. Turn left on Cuvier Street and left onto Prospect Street. You'll now be at the **Museum of Contemporary Art** (see p36). Check out the exhibits or have a snack in the café.

Louis Gill designed the original museum and the older architecture in this area. Walk back toward the village and peek inside **780 Prospect St**; the cottage dates back to 1904. Cross Prospect at Fay but keep on Prospect. Pass through the Arcade Building to Girard Avenue. Turn right and window-shop along La Jolla's main street. Of note is **Warwick's** at 7812, a stationer and bookstore, and **R. B. Stevenson Gallery**, Girard Avenue. Go north on Girard for a block and a half, and then finish your walk with one of the freshly baked delights at **Girard Gourmet** (see p105).

See map on p98

Coast Highway 101

1 The Flower Fields
MAP D1 ■ 5704 Paseo del Norte, Carlsbad ■ Adm

In spring, the hillsides explode with brilliant-colored blossoms of the giant tecolote ranunculus. The Carlsbad Ranch harvests 6–8 million bulbs for export.

2 LEGOLAND®
MAP D1 ■ 1 Legoland Dr, Carlsbad ■ (760) 918-5346 ■ Adm

This theme park and aquarium is devoted to the plastic brick. Kids enjoy the hands-on activities, waterpark, and models *(see p58)*.

3 Del Mar
MAP D2

The wealthiest community among North County's beach towns, Del Mar is filled with sidewalk cafés and shops.

4 Solana Beach
MAP D2

At this popular beach town, Cedros Design District shops and cafés are two blocks from Fletcher Cove; check with lifeguards before you swim.

5 Cardiff-by-the-Sea
MAP D2

Surfers enjoy the reef break at Cardiff, while RV campers kick back at a beachside campground. The San Elijo Lagoon offers hiking trails through an ecological reserve.

San Diego Botanic Garden, Encinitas

6 Leucadia
MAP D2

The 21st century hasn't yet hit this sleepy town with a small beach and shops, restaurants, and galleries.

7 Carlsbad
MAP D1

In the 1880s, Captain John Frazier discovered that the water here had the same mineral content as a spa in Karlsbad, Bohemia. Today, this pretty village still draws visitors with its beaches, resorts, and shops.

8 Oceanside
MAP D1 ■ California Surf Museum: 312 Pier View Way; (760) 721-6876; open 10am–4pm daily; adm

Town fortunes are tied with adjoining Camp Pendleton. The California Surf Museum shows a history of the sport.

9 Camp Pendleton
MAP D1

Endangered species and abundant wildlife thrive at the largest US Marine Corps base and amphibious training facility in the country.

10 Encinitas
MAP D2 ■ Self-Realization Fellowship Retreat and Hermitage: 215 W. K St ■ San Diego Botanic Garden: 230 Quail Gardens Dr; adm

Highlights in Encinitas include the Self-Realization Fellowship Retreat and Hermitage and the San Diego Botanic Garden *(see p100)*.

Shopping

1 San Diego Botanic Garden Gift Shops
MAP D2 ▪ 230 Quail Gardens Drive, Encinitas ▪ (760) 436-3036

Set in a public garden with more than 4,000 plant species from around the world, these shops sell unique home and garden decor, books, locally made jewelry and more. There's also a selection of plants, most propagated from species found in the garden.

San Diego Botanic Garden Shops

2 Self-Realization Fellowship Encinitas Books & Gifts
MAP D2 ▪ 1150 South Coast Highway 101, Encinitas ▪ (760) 753-5353 ▪ Closed Mon & hols

In addition to books and music featuring SRF founder Paramahansa Yogananda and others, this elegant store sells scarves, jewelry and gifts.

3 Chino
MAP D2 ▪ 6123 Calzada del Bosque, Rancho Santa Fe ▪ (858) 756-3184

The Chino family farm and its store cater to famous chefs and lovers of superb fruit and vegetables.

4 Encinitas Seaside Bazaar
MAP D2 ▪ 459 South Coast Highway 101, Encinitas ▪ (760) 753-1611

This year-round open-air market offers unique antiques and home decor, arts and crafts, and various other delightful surprises.

5 Fresh Produce
MAP N2 ▪ 1147 Prospect St, La Jolla ▪ (858) 456-8134

Colorful, comfy womenswear epitomizes the region's laid-back lifestyle. The pieces here flatter most shapes and sizes. Also stocked are bags, hats, and other seaside needs.

6 Trader Joe's
MAP A3 ▪ 1211 Garnet Ave, Pacific Beach ▪ (858) 272-7235

This market sells imaginative salads, a wide variety of cheeses, wine, and fun ethnic food that you won't find in a regular supermarket.

7 Carlsbad Premium Outlets
MAP D1 ▪ 5620 Paseo del Norte, Carlsbad

Shop for bargains in one of the most pleasant outlet centers around. Gap, Bass, Salvatore Ferragamo, and Jones New York are all here.

8 Cedros Design District
MAP D2 ▪ Cedros Ave, Solana Beach

This former warehouse district has been transformed into a shopping street full of design stores, furnishings, and boutiques. The 100 shops at the Leaping Lotus offer ethnic goods, clothing, and furniture.

9 Del Mar Plaza
MAP D2 ▪ 1555 Camino Del Mar, Del Mar

Italian home accessories, estate art, and well-known chains such as Banana Republic and White House/Black Market can be found here.

10 Winery Gift Shops
MAP E1

Most wineries in Temecula operate gift shops that stock unusual cookbooks, entertaining supplies, and home decor items. Additionally, many have delis where you can find picnic food to accompany that bottle of wine you just bought.

See map on p98

Cafés and Bars

Belly Up Tavern

1 Belly Up Tavern
MAP D2 ▪ 143 S. Cedros Ave, Solana Beach ▪ (858) 481-9022 ▪ Adm

One of the best live music venues in the county. Old Quonset huts have been acoustically altered to showcase bands.

2 Encinitas Ale House
MAP D2 ▪ 1044 S. Coast Hwy 101, Encinitas ▪ (760) 943-7180 ▪ $$

Popular for burgers and ales, this cozy place has 32 taps rotating Belgian and German beers, craft beers, and international microbrews.

3 Wild Note Café
MAP D2 ▪ 143 S. Cedros Ave, Solana Beach ▪ (858) 720-9000 ▪ $

Come here for lunch, served outside or under structural beams. Dinner-times tend to be hectic.

4 Brockton Villa
MAP N2 ▪ 1235 Coast Blvd, La Jolla ▪ (858) 454-7393 ▪ No dis. access ▪ $$

This historic place offers breakfast, lunch, or dinner, and fabulous views. Choices include seafood and steak.

5 Pannikin
MAP D2 ▪ 510 N. Coast Hwy 101, Encinitas ▪ (760) 436-5824 ▪ $

Don't miss this coffeehouse inside a Santa Fe Railroad Depot. Sit upstairs or outside on a shady deck.

6 Living Room Coffeehouse
MAP N2 ▪ 1010 Prospect St ▪ (858) 459-1187 ▪ $

Grab a back table at this hip coffeehouse in upscale La Jolla to enjoy a million-dollar view.

7 Ruby's Diner
MAP D1 ▪ 1 Oceanside Pier, Oceanside ▪ (760) 433-7829 ▪ $

Walk 1,942 ft (591 m) out to the pier's end and order a salad or burger and a malt at this 1940s-style diner.

8 VG Donut & Bakery
MAP D2 ▪ 106 Aberdeen Drive, Cardiff ▪ (760) 753-2400 ▪ $

This local favorite offers dozens of variations of wedding cakes, pastries, bear claws, bagels, fresh hot donuts, cookies, and much more.

9 Lotus Café and Juice Bar
MAP D2 ▪ 765 S. Coast Hwy 101, Encinitas ▪ (760) 479-1977 ▪ $

Lotus is especially appealing to vegetarian and vegan diners, but meat dishes are also offered. Juices are freshly squeezed.

10 Lean and Green Café
MAP N3 ▪ 7825 Fay Ave, Suite 180, La Jolla ▪ (858) 459-5326 ▪ $

The organic offerings here include wraps, salads, and smoothies, as well as vegan and gluten-free items.

Places to Eat

1 Del Mar Rendezvous
MAP D2 ■ 1555 Camino Del Mar, Suite 102, Del Mar ■ (858) 755-2669 ■ Closed Thanksgiving Day & Super Bowl Sun ■ $$

Book in advance for this popular modern Chinese restaurant, which also lists more than 100 wines.

2 Poseidon
MAP D2 ■ 1670 Coast Blvd, Del Mar ■ Closed Thanksgiving & Christmas Days ■ (858) 755-9345 ■ $$

The patio here is great for lunch, dinner, weekend brunch, and cocktails at sunset.

3 Eddie V's Prime Seafood
MAP N2 ■ 1270 Prospect St, La Jolla ■ (858) 459-5500 ■ $$$

Fresh seafood and meat dishes. Every table has a view of La Jolla Cove, and there's live jazz nightly (see p65).

A plate of food at Eddie V's Prime Seafood

4 101 Café
MAP D1 ■ 631 S. Coast Hwy, Oceanside ■ (760) 722-5220 ■ $

Since its 1928 beginnings as a roadside diner, folks passing through have enjoyed the home-style comfort food.

5 The Cottage
MAP N3 ■ 7702 Fay Ave, La Jolla ■ (858) 454-8409 ■ $$

At this lovely, quiet 1900s bungalow, the patio is the perfect place to enjoy a light breakfast or lunch.

6 Girard Gourmet
MAP N2 ■ 7837 Girard Ave, La Jolla ■ (858) 454-3321 ■ $

Choose salads, entrées, or sandwiches. And try a designer cookie!

7 Sushi Ota
MAP B3 ■ 4529 Mission Bay Dr ■ (858) 270-5670 ■ $$

Considered the best sushi in town, connoisseurs come to Sushi Ota

PRICE CATEGORIES
Price categories include a three-course meal for one, half a bottle of wine, and all unavoidable extra charges including tax.

$ under $40 $$ $40–$80 $$$ over $80

for the day's freshest fish transformed into tasty works of art (see p64).

8 Rubio's
MAP B3 ■ 4504 E. Mission Bay Dr ■ (858) 272-2801 ■ $

At the first of a hugely successful Mexican fast-food chain, enjoy the best fish tacos this side of Baja.

9 Mille Fleurs
MAP D2 ■ 6009 Paseo Delicias, Rancho Santa Fe ■ (858) 756-3085 ■ $$$

The most acclaimed restaurant in San Diego County provides a culinary feast. Fireplaces, fresh flowers, and tapestries complement the exquisite and beautifully presented food.

Mille Fleurs

10 Vigilucci's Cucina Italiana
MAP D1 ■ 2943 State St, Carlsbad ■ (760) 434-2500 ■ $$

Classic antipasti, soups, and substantial servings of pastas and entrées are crowd-pleasers here, as is the daily happy hour.

See map on p98

Streetsmart

**A cart displaying goods for sale
at the Old Town Market**

Getting To and Around San Diego

Arriving by Air

San Diego International Airport (SAN), also known as Lindbergh Field, is only 3 miles (5 km) northwest of downtown San Diego. **Alaska Airlines**, **Frontier Airlines**, and **Southwest Airlines** operate from Terminal 1, with all other airlines at Terminal 2. The free Airport Loop shuttle bus connects the two terminals. The only non-stop international flights are to and from Canada, Mexico, Japan, and the UK.

Taxis and door-to-door shuttles may be found at the Transportation Plaza, accessible to Terminal 1 via a skybridge and to Terminal 2 directly across the street by exiting baggage claim. Just outside baggage claim, bus route 992 takes approximately 10 minutes to downtown San Diego. It stops at the corner of W. Broadway and Kettner, which is directly across the street from the **Santa Fe Depot** (**Amtrak** and the **Coaster**) and **America Plaza** (trolley). Buses run every 15 minutes from 5am to 11:30pm on weekdays and every 30 minutes on weekends.

Tijuana International Airport is located 5 miles (8 km) east of downtown Tijuana, with frequent flights to the rest of Mexico, as well as direct flights to and from China and Japan. Domestic flights within Mexico are often cheaper than flying internationally from California. If you are a ticketed passenger, a fee-based pedestrian bridge to

the border is a 5-minute walk from baggage claim. After immigration, shuttles are available to San Ysidro (every 30 minutes from 5am to 2am) or the Santa Fe Depot (every 2 hours from 5:30am to 1:30am).

Check **SuperShuttle**'s website for more information on shuttles.

Arriving by Train

Amtrak's Pacific Surfliners arrive at the historic Santa Fe Depot. About 11 trains travel daily to and from Orange County and Los Angeles, and several continue on to Santa Barbara.

Arriving by Road

Greyhound buses cover the entire US and most of Canada. There are direct connections from Los Angeles, with many continuing to the border and Tijuana's central bus terminal. A few daily buses go directly to Phoenix.

By car from Los Angeles, I-5 passes along coastal towns, heads into downtown, and continues to the international border at San Ysidro. Shortly before La Jolla, I-5 splits with I-805, reconnecting at the border. If driving from the east, I-8 passes through Mission Valley and ends just past SeaWorld. I-15 from Las Vegas serves inland San Diego County.

Arriving by Cruise Ship

All cruise ships moor at B Street Terminal along

the Embarcadero on N. Harbor Drive within easy walking distance of downtown. Popular sailings include the Mexican Riviera or mini-cruises to Ensenada and Catalina. A number of ships sail to and from Canada and Alaska, Hawaii, and Panama.

Traveling by Bus and Trolley

Public transport will take you just about anywhere in San Diego. City buses connect with the **North County Transit District**, which serves coastal and inland San Diego County. Inexpensive and fun, the red trolley is a light-rail system with three lines. The Blue line travels between downtown's America Plaza and the Mexican border at San Ysidro. The Green line is handy for the Gaslamp Quarter, the Convention Center, and Seaport Village. The Orange line crosses downtown and continues out to El Cajon. Buses and trolleys operate from 4:30am until midnight.

You can only buy tickets on the bus with exact change. Single adult fares are $2.25, except for express buses. Single adult trolley tickets are $2.50, valid for 2 hours. Vending machines sell trolley tickets at each stop. No transfers are allowed between buses and trolleys. If you plan to hop on and off buses and trolleys, 1- to 4-day, and 14-day passes are available but only with a Compass Card. Reloadable Compass Cards may be purchased for $2 at The Transit Store and Albertson's and Vons supermarkets throughout San Diego.

By Train

A regional commuter rail service runs daily between the Santa Fe Depot and Oceanside. You can buy tickets at vending machines at stations and use them for 2 hours after purchase.

By Taxi

Taxis don't cruise for fares. You can usually find a taxi stand in front of large hotels, the airport, and some shopping centers. Rates are posted on the taxi door; distances in San Diego can make some trips expensive. **Uber** services are very popular and arguably more affordable.

By Water Taxi

On-call water taxis will transport you to locations around the harbor. They run from Friday to Sunday, noon to 10pm.

By Ferry

Flagship Cruises operates a service between San Diego and Coronado. Ferries depart from Broadway Pier at 990 N. Harbor Drive and the Convention Center Marina. From Coronado, ferries leave from the Coronado Ferry Landing, 1201 First Street. Ferries leave hourly from 9am to 9pm (to 10pm on Friday and Saturday). One-way fares are $4.75.

By Bicycle

The greater San Diego region has over 1,300 miles (2,090 km) of bikeways. Public bicycles may be rented on an hourly basis or unlimited usage with a monthly membership. **The Bike Revolution**, **Deco Bike** and **Stay Classy Bike Rentals** all offer good deals.

By Car

You won't need a car in downtown San Diego, but it's essential to get around the rest of the city or region. A few car-rental agencies also have cars you can drive into Mexico, but you will need to agree this with your agent before traveling and buy additional insurance at the border. These include **Budget** and **California Baja Rent-a-Car**.

DIRECTORY

ARRIVING BY AIR

Alaska Airlines
ᵂ alaskaair.com

Frontier Airlines
ᵂ flyfrontier.com

San Diego International Airport
ᵂ san.org

Southwest Airlines
ᵂ southwest.com

Tijuana International Airport
ᵂ tijuana-airport.com

ARRIVING BY TRAIN

Amtrak
ᵂ amtrak.com

Coaster
ᵂ gonctd.com

Santa Fe Depot
MAP H4 ▪ 1050 Kettner Blvd

ARRIVING BY ROAD

Greyhound
MAP L6 ▪ 1313 National Avenue
ᵂ greyhound.com

BUS AND TROLLEY

America Plaza
MAP H4 ▪ Kettner Blvd & W. Broadway

North County Transit District
ᵂ gonctd.com

San Diego Metropolitan Transit System
ᵂ sdmts.com

TAXIS, LIMOUSINES, SHUTTLES, AND WATER TAXIS

San Diego Taxi Company
📞 (619) 566-6666

San Diego Water Taxi
📞 (619) 234-4411

SuperShuttle
📞 (800) 258-3826
ᵂ supershuttle.com

Uber
ᵂ uber.com

TRAVELING BY FERRY

Flagship Cruises
ᵂ flagshipsd.com/cruises/coronado-ferry

BICYCLE RENTALS

The Bike Revolution
ᵂ thebikerevolution.com

Deco Bike
ᵂ decobike.com

Stay Classy Bike Rentals
ᵂ stayclassybikes.com

TRAVELING BY CAR

Budget
ᵂ locations.budget.com/us/ca/san-diego/san.html

California Baja Rent-a-Car
ᵂ cabaja.com/usa-rentals

Practical Information

Passports and Visas

All visitors to the US must have a valid passport. Citizens of 38 countries may enter without a visa under the Visa Waiver Program for stays of up to 90 days. To use this program, you must have an e-passport embedded with an electronic chip; prior to travel, apply for eligibility through the Electronic System for Travel Authorization (**ESTA**). On arrival in the US, a Customs and Border Protection officer will make the final determination to allow entry.

Customs and Immigration

If clearing customs and immigration at San Diego International Airport, the process is straightforward. If crossing at the San Ysidro International Border, expect long lines and additional scrutiny if you've come from the interior of Mexico.

Everyone above the age of 21 is allowed 1 liter of liquor and 200 cigarettes duty free. Citizens may bring in $400 worth of gifts; non-citizens, $100. Cash exceeding $10,000 must be declared. Fresh produce, meats, plants, and products from endangered species are prohibited.

Travel Safety Advice

Visitors can get up-to-date travel safety information from the **Foreign and Commonwealth Office** in the UK, the **State Department** in the US, and the **Department of Foreign Affairs and Trade** in Australia.

Travel Insurance

Be sure to obtain comprehensive travel insurance before arriving in the US; this will cover you for trip interruptions, lost baggage, and some limited medical expenses. If coming from abroad, always check with your primary healthcare insurer at home to see if you have any coverage while in the US. An international medical insurance policy is a good idea to protect you against the unexpected. Although you won't be denied medical care if you fall ill in the US, you can expect a staggeringly large bill.

If renting a car, establish what your auto insurer and credit card company covers in case of accident or theft. An auto insurance policy is not valid in Mexico; if you plan on driving there it's important to buy Mexican insurance before you cross over the border.

Health

Enjoy the brilliant sunshine, but slather on the sunscreen during the day, and be sure to take a hat whenever you're outdoors. California has one of the country's highest incidences of skin cancer – no surprise since people pursue outdoor activities year round.

Ocean waters are generally clean, except after a heavy storm; accumulated and untreated runoff from miles away washes down storm drains and empties into the ocean, and sewer leaks are common.

Smoking is forbidden inside any public enclosed area, including restaurants and bars. The city of San Diego has banned smoking on beaches and in parks and open spaces.

San Diego has some of the country's best hospitals. If your situation is not life threatening, urgent-care clinics are less expensive. If you don't have health insurance, head to a community clinic. Expect to pay on the spot for services rendered. Many pharmacies throughout the city, such as CVS, Rite-Aid, and Walgreens, are open 24 hours.

Emergency Services

During an emergency, dial 911 from any telephone. Be prepared to specify your location and whether medical and/or police assistance is needed. Call the police department for all other matters.

Personal Security

San Diego is a safe city; most petty crime is limited to theft and car break-ins. Common sense prevails: don't walk around late at night, and don't leave valuables inside your car. San Diego's proximity to the Mexican border makes car theft a concern – if your car is found across the border, the paperwork to bring it back is overwhelming. Neighborhoods prone to theft include Pacific Beach, San Ysidro, and Mission Valley.

Dangerous riptides can occur along the coastal beaches; ask lifeguards about swimming conditions at unfamiliar beaches. Posted green flags indicate safe swimming, yellow mean caution, and red flags denote hazardous surf. If you are caught in a riptide, let the current carry you down the coast until it dies out, then swim in to the shore.

Lost Property

San Diego International Airport has a **Lost and Found** department. If you have lost an item on the transit system, call **The Transit Store**. Items of value will be transferred to the police department after a set time.

Women Travelers

San Diego is safe for women travelers, but lone females should always be alert to their surroundings, especially after dark. Don't walk on the beach alone at night, be careful in parking lots, take the usual precautions at hotels, and control alcohol intake.

Disabled Travelers

The excellent booklet *Access in San Diego*, published by **Accessible San Diego**, gives specific access information on many hotels, restaurants, and shopping centers. Also included are public and private transportation

firms equipped with lifts, and car rental agencies that offer hand-controlled vehicles. You'll also find a directory of medical equipment suppliers and disability organizations.

All buses, trolleys, and the Coaster are equipped with lifts. Amtrak trains have limited accessible spaces and recommend advance reservations. Greyhound provides a lift-equipped bus with advance notice. Super Shuttle *(see p109)* provides transport-ation from the airport, also with advance notice.

If driving your own car, reserved parking spaces are marked by a blue curb, a blue-and-white wheelchair logo on the pavement, and by a posted sign. You may park for free in most metered areas, but a special disabled permit must be displayed.

Every intersection and sidewalk in San Diego has ramped curbs or at least a ramped driveway. Ramped access is standard in government buildings, museums, some theaters, and large hotels and restaurants.

Hotels with more than five rooms must provide accessible accommodation to disabled guests. It is best to call in advance to reserve one of these rooms, and specify if you need a roll-in shower. When making restaurant reservations, do clarify that you require access.

Imperial Beach, Ocean Beach, Coronado, Mission Beach, Oceanside, Silver Strand State Beach, and La Jolla Shores have power and manual beach chairs. These are free to use, but it's best to book ahead.

DIRECTORY

PASSPORTS AND VISAS

ESTA
w esta.cbp.dhs.gov

TRAVEL SAFETY INFORMATION

Australia
Department of Foreign Affairs and Trade
w dfat.gov.au
w smartraveller.gov.au

UK
Foreign and Commonwealth Office
w gov.uk/foreign-travel-advice

US
US Department of State
w travel.state.gov

EMERGENCY NUMBERS

Medical or Police Assistance
(911

Rape Crisis Hotline
((888) 385-4657

San Diego Police Department
((619) 531-2000

24-HOUR EMERGENCY ROOMS

Scripps Hospital La Jolla
((858) 457-4123

Scripps Mercy Hospital
((619) 294-8111

LOST PROPERTY

Airport Lost and Found
((619) 400-2141

The Transit Store
((619) 234-1060

DISABLED TRAVELERS

Accessible San Diego
((619) 325-7550
w access-sandiego.org

Currency and Banking

Paper bills are in denominations of $1, $5, $10, $20, $50, and $100. Rare but still in circulation are paper bills of $2. Coins are 1¢, 5¢, 10¢, 25¢, 50¢, and $1. The $1 coins have a slight gold cast to them and are slightly larger and heavier than a 25¢ coin. If paying for anything in cash with a merchant, expect to have any paper bills larger than a $20 scrutinized.

San Diego International Airport has international exchange kiosks in Terminal 1 and Terminal 2. **Travelex** has two other locations in Horton Plaza and Fashion Valley. Major banks handle most transactions, but you will need to bring plenty of ID. Large hotels exchange currency as well, but offer low rates. Exchange windows in San Ysidro handle transactions in dollars and pesos.

There are 24-hour automatic teller machines (ATMs) all over the city. Look on the back of your bank card or credit card to see which network it's associated with. ATMs inside convenience stores or malls charge you for use, as does your own bank if you go outside the network.

Most major banks are found throughout San Diego. Banking hours are usually 9am or 10am until 6pm, Monday through Friday, with Saturday hours from 9am to 1pm or 2pm.

Visa and **MasterCard** credit and debit cards are widely accepted, **Diners Club** and **American Express** cards slightly less so. If using a non-US-issued credit card, make sure it has a magnetic strip on the back, since chip-and-pin readers are not common.

Telephone and Internet

Coin telephones are hard to find in San Diego, but they still exist at San Diego International Airport, transit stations, hospitals, some hotels and restaurants, and government buildings. You may dial emergency services on 911 without coins from any of these phones. If you carry an unlocked phone, you can find SIM cards with a variety of prepaid, no-contract plans at supermarkets, corner stores, Target, and Walmart. T-Mobile and AT&T stores also carry SIM cards. There are free Wi-Fi hotspots all over the city: in cafés, fast-food restaurants, and even in Horton Plaza shopping center. Public libraries also have computer terminals to use, as do hostels, but you must be a guest. Most hotels offer free Wi-Fi, as does San Diego International Airport but in 30-minute sessions.

Postal Services

Regular post office hours are 8:30am–5pm Monday to Friday, with some branches open on Saturday mornings. Stamps are usually available from vending machines in the lobby, and signage indicates the cost of postage for mail sent to domestic and international addresses. Stamps are available at many supermarkets and franchised mail service stores, which also provide shipping services. Hotel concierges can post mail for you. **FedEx** and **UPS** offer courier services with guaranteed overnight delivery and reliable international service. Many of their franchise offices sell packaging supplies. Much cheaper, the US Postal Service offers overnight service in the continental US and two- and three-day services internationally.

Television, Radio, and Newspapers

All four major US television networks have affiliate local channels in San Diego (**10 news** for ABC, **CBS 8** for CBS, **Fox 5 San Diego** for Fox and **NBC 7 San Diego** for NBC). Public broadcasting is represented as well.

Local news and talk radio stations include **KOGO**, **KFMB** and **KPBS**. The morning local newscast traffic reports can be particularly useful. Try to listen to them before you head out in the morning and you may save yourself from a massive traffic jam.

Newspapers are available in stands throughout the city. The daily *San Diego Union Tribune* is strong in regional news on both sides of the border. The *San Diego Reader* is the best source of the latest happenings in town. You'll find details of movies and theater timings, and music events. Free copies can be found all over the city.

Opening Hours

Most museums are open from 10am to 5pm. Check the website or call before making plans, as many close one day of the week. Retail shops usually open at 10am and close at 5pm or 6pm. Regular hours at shopping malls are 10am–9pm Mon–Sat and 11am–7pm Sun. Department stores sometimes open at 7am for super-sales or extend their hours during the holiday season. Malls close only during a few major holidays, such as Christmas and New Year; however, some stores may be open on Thanksgiving (the fourth Thursday in November) and Easter Sunday.

You shouldn't have any trouble finding 24-hour convenience stores, gas stations, drug stores, and supermarkets. A few Walmarts and Targets in San Diego are also open 24 hours.

Time Difference

From the first Sunday in November until the second Sunday in March, San Diego operates on Pacific Standard Time (PST), which is 8 hours behind Greenwich Mean Time (GMT). For the remaining months, the clock moves ahead 1 hour and becomes Pacific Daylight Time (PDT), or 7 hours behind Greenwich Mean Time.

Electrical Appliances

The US uses plugs with two flat blades and sometimes a third round grounding pin. Either type will fit in American sockets. Power is set at 110 volts, so 220-volt-only appliances will not work efficiently, and a power converter will be necessary. Small appliances like hairdryers or curling irons are inexpensive to buy at discount stores, and hotels usually provide hairdryers. Most modern electronics are designed to work on either the 110 or 220 system; however, if coming from abroad, you will need a plug adapter. It might be easier to buy this at home before coming to the US.

Most adapters sold in US stores are just for Americans traveling abroad. If you do forget to bring an adapter, you can usually find one in a Best Buy store.

Weather

San Diego enjoys the most temperate climate in the nation. The rainy season usually begins in December, with a few large storms rolling in by spring. Winter days can be warm and sunny, but ocean temperatures are cold. Late spring often presents what locals call "May gray" and "June gloom." During this time, you often find a lot of low cloud cover, but you can just as easily get endless days of dazzling sunshine. Sometimes you might find a rare, mild summer shower. Summer evenings are pleasant but often cool, so make sure you bring a sweater or lightweight jacket with you. During the summer months, be aware that if you leave the coast and head inland the temperatures are considerably warmer.

DIRECTORY

CURRENCY AND BANKING

American Express
((800) 528-4800

Diners Club
((800) 234-6377

MasterCard
((800) 627-8372

Travelex
w travelex.com

Visa
((800) 847-2911

COURIER SERVICES

FedEx
w fedex.com

UPS
w ups.com

TELEVISION, RADIO, AND NEWSPAPERS

10 news
w 10news.com

CBS 8
w cbs8.com

Fox 5 San Diego
w fox5sandiego.com

KFMB
760 KFMB-AM

KOGO
600 KOGO-AM

KPBS
89.5 KPBS-FM

NBC 7 San Diego
w nbcsandiego.com

San Diego Reader
w sandiegoreader.com

San Diego Union Tribune
w sandiegounion-
tribune.com

Visitor Information

Before you travel, order a copy of the *San Diego Visitors Planning Guide* from the **San Diego Tourism Authority** website. You may view past copies online. You'll also find links to download mobile apps for La Jolla *(see pp36–7)*, Little Italy *(see p78)*, and other attractions and museums. Once you're in San Diego, stop by the **San Diego Visitor Information Center** at the Embarcadero, where staff will answer your questions about activities and tours. They also sell tickets to attractions. The **Coronado Visitor Center** can give you a map of Coronado and suggest activities in the area.

Excursions and City Tours

Old Town Trolley Tours makes 11 stops in a continuous 2-hour loop around San Diego's most popular attractions, including Old Town, the Embarcadero, Seaport Village, Horton Plaza, Gaslamp Quarter, Coronado, Balboa Park, and Little Italy. From Old Town, tours depart at 9am and every 30 minutes until late afternoon, depending on the time of year. Departure times vary from each stop. The tours are narrated and drivers are quite knowledgeable. Adult tickets are $39 ($35.10 online), and you can hop on and hop off as you please. The same company operates San Diego SEAL tours, which uses a type of amphibious vehicle to first tour the

streets of the city before it enters San Diego Bay to power past Navy vessels and harbor sights, and La Jolla and Mission Beach tours.

Five Star Tours operates bus tours to popular attractions throughout San Diego County, including Legoland, San Diego Safari Park, wine tours, city tours, and a number of trips to Tijuana and Ensenada, Mexico.

San Diego Scenic Tours offers half- and full-day narrated tours on air-conditioned buses or mini-buses around San Diego, the harbor, and Tijuana (passports are required).

Flagship Cruises *(see p109)* offers several ways to tour the harbor. There are 1- and 2-hour narrated trips covering the harbor, Shelter Island, Point Loma, Coronado Bridge, and more. Dinner, nature, and whale-watching cruises are also available.

Walking tours – like those organized by **Balboa Park Tours** and **Coronado Walking Tour** – are also very popular.

Shopping

You don't have to go far to find something to buy in San Diego. Shopping malls are everywhere, with the same stores as every shopping mall in the country. The best bargains can be found around public holidays. San Diego has three major outlet centers within an hour's driving distance: the **Carlsbad Premium Outlets** in North County, the **Las Americas Premium Outlets** at San Ysidro, and **Viejas Outlet Center**

on the Viejas Indian Reservation, east on I-8. You can usually find good deals at the designer spin-off shops. Upscale boutiques are located in La Jolla, and if you're looking for unusual gifts, the museum shops in Balboa Park *(see p81)* are a good starting point. Current sales tax in San Diego County is 8 percent. A non-refundable sales tax is added to all retail purchases.

Dining

With its proximity to the Pacific Ocean, Mexico, and surrounding ranch and farmlands, you won't go hungry in San Diego. The Gaslamp Quarter is packed with restaurants, but many are overcrowded and on the noisy side. Foodies tend to go to restaurants in Little Italy or Bankers Hill. For romantic dining with an ocean view, La Jolla offers the city's best choices. Prices of entrées in the more popular tourist areas match those of any urban area. You'll find affordable ethnic restaurants everywhere, with some of the more interesting choices in the Hillcrest neighborhood. If traveling with kids, the best family-friendly restaurants are in Mission Valley and Mission Bay.

On weekends throughout the year and during the summer months, it's wise to make a reservation. Some of the better restaurants can be bought out for a private event, so call ahead rather than just show up. Lunch hours are usually 11am to 2pm or 3pm, with dinner service beginning at 5pm or 5:30pm and kitchens closing at 10pm. Dress is casual everywhere. Most food servers expect a 15–20 percent tip; leave it in cash, or add it to your credit card bill. With large parties, an 18 percent gratuity may be automatically added to the check.

Entrées on the lunch menu are often less than half the price of those at dinner. Some restaurants offer early-bird dinners from 4pm until 6pm, with a limited number of discounted entrées. Many restaurants and bars offer happy hours on weekdays. For the price of a drink and a few dollars, you can snack on anything from a hot buffet to chips and dip. Some Mexican restaurants sell inexpensive tacos on "Taco Tuesdays." Check out the advertisements in the San Diego Reader.

The legal drinking age in California is 21. If you look under 30, restaurant servers and merchants will ask to see your photo identification. In Tijuana, the legal drinking age is 18.

Where to Stay

No matter your budget, you'll find something in San Diego – from the ultra-posh to the humble dormitory-style hostel. Given the city's popularity, be sure to make your reservations early to avoid frustration.

Staying at a motel chain like **Days Inn** or **Motel 6** offers standardized accommodations with no surprises. Most major chains can be found in Mission Valley's Hotel Circle. Parking is generally free, breakfast is often provided, and you aren't charged countless petty fees.

If you plan to stay in San Diego for more than a few weeks, consider renting an apartment. Keep in mind that summer rentals, especially along the beach, are more costly. Be sure to ask what amenities are included.

You can always find accommodations on online booking sites such as **Booking.com** and **Airbnb**, but it's important to read the reviews, which are written by bona fide guests, carefully. Sometimes the price is right but the location is remote.

The only comfortable place to camp legally near the city is in **San Diego Metro KOA**. This well-located campground offers a swimming pool, hot tub, and bicycle rentals. RV owners can try **Campland on the Bay**, which also accepts tent campers.

DIRECTORY

VISITOR INFORMATION

Coronado Visitor Center
MAP C6 ▪ 1100 Orange Ave, Coronado
📞 (619) 437-8788
🔳 coronado
visitorcenter.com

San Diego Tourism Authority
🔳 sandiego.org

San Diego Visitor Information Center
MAP J6 ▪ 996 N. Harbor Drive
📞 (619) 737-2999
🔳 sandiegovisit.org

EXCURSIONS AND CITY TOURS

Balboa Park Tours
🔳 balboapark.org/visit/tours

Coronado Walking Tour
🔳 coronadowalking
tour.com

Five Star Tours
🔳 sdsuntours.com

Old Town Trolley Tours
🔳 trolleytours.com/
san-diego

San Diego Scenic Tours
🔳 sandiegoscenictours.
com

SHOPPING

Las Americas Premium Outlets
🔳 premiumoutlets.com/
outlet/las-americas

Carlsbad Premium Outlets
🔳 premiumoutlets.com/
outlet/Carlsbad

Viejas Outlets Center
🔳 viejas.com/

san-diegos-premier-
outlet-mall

WHERE TO STAY

Airbnb
🔳 airbnb.com

Booking.com
🔳 booking.com

Days Inn
🔳 daysinn.com

Motel 6
🔳 motel6.com

CAMPING

Campland On the Bay
MAP B3 ▪ 2211 Pacific Beach Dr
🔳 campland.com

San Diego Metro KOA
111 N. 2nd Ave, Chula Vista
🔳 koa.com/
campgrounds/san-diego

Places to Stay

PRICE CATEGORIES
For a standard, double room per night (with breakfast if included), taxes, and extra charges.

$ under $200 $$ $200–$300 $$$ over $300

Luxury Hotels

L'Auberge Del Mar Resort & Spa
MAP D2 ■ 1540 Camino del Mar, Del Mar ■ (858) 259-1515 ■ www.lauberge delmar.com ■ $$
Join the list of Hollywood notables who relax at this boutique hotel and spa near the Pacific. The rooms have marble baths and many include private balconies and fireplaces.

La Casa del Zorro Resort & Spa
MAP F2 3845 Yaqui Pass Road, Borrego Springs ■ (760) 767-0100 ■ www. lacasadelzorro.com ■ $$
This classic desert resort offers poolside rooms and private casitas, featuring wood-burning fireplaces and marble bathtubs. Facilities include a spa, fitness center, three swimming pools, and tennis courts. Conditions for stargazing in the night desert sky are perfect.

Coronado Island Marriott Resort and Spa
MAP C6 ■ 2000 2nd St, Coronado ■ (619) 435-3000 ■ www.marriott. com/sanci ■ $$
Lush grounds with a relaxed feel, and dedicated staff make this hotel a top choice. Californian and French styling prevails, with the best of the rooms looking out across the bay to San Diego. The hotel also runs a watertaxi service.

Estancia La Jolla Hotel & Spa
MAP A1 9700 N. Torrey Pines Rd ■ (858) 550-1000 ■ www.estancialajolla. com ■ $$
Elegant and airy rooms offer luxury and comfort in this Spanish ranch-style hotel surrounded by lush gardens. Indulge yourself at the spa or heated saltwater pool. A short walk leads down to the beach.

Rancho Bernardo Inn
MAP E2 ■ 17550 Bernardo Oaks Dr, Rancho Bernardo ■ (877) 517-9340 ■ www.rancho bernardoinn.com ■ $$
Red-tile-roof adobe buildings and bougainvillea-adorned patios evoke images of early California at this relaxing resort set in stunning grounds. Life here revolves around the adjoining golf course, spa, and tennis courts.

Fairmont Grand Del Mar
MAP E2 ■ 5300 Grand Del Mar Court ■ (858) 314-2000 ■ www.fairmont. com/san-diego ■ $$$
Discover the inland beauty of San Diego at this stunning Spanish- and Italian-style destination resort. Luxurious rooms with fine amenities, superb service, golf, pools, spa, hiking trails, and equestrian facilities are reasons never to leave.

Four Seasons Residence Club Aviara
MAP D2 ■ 7210 Blue Heron Place ■ (760) 603-3700 ■ vacationrentals. fourseasons.com ■ $$$
With impeccable service and a superb setting, this property offers luxurious residential rentals. Choose between indoor and out-door treatment rooms, or a suite with a whirlpool.

Hard Rock Hotel
MAP K6 ■ 207 5th Avenue ■ (619) 702-3000 ■ www. hardrockhotelsd.com ■ $$$
The contemporary rooms and suites at this hotel look out across the Gaslamp Quarter. The atmosphere is lively, and friendly staff will cater to your needs, even loaning you a Fender guitar.

Hotel Solamar
MAP K5 ■ 435 6th Ave ■ (619) 819-9500 ■ www. hotelsolamar.com ■ $$$
This hip boutique hotel in the Gaslamp Quarter offers a complimentary wine hour every evening in the fireplace lounge. California cuisine features at the JSix restaurant, and the fourth-floor pool deck with J6Bar and fire pits is pop-ular with the locals, too.

The Lodge at Torrey Pines
MAP D2 ■ 11480 N. Torrey Pines Rd, La Jolla ■ (858) 453-4420 ■ www.lodge torreypines.com ■ $$$
Located on the cliffs of Torrey Pines, this

lodge offers exquisite accommodations. The rooms look out onto a courtyard that reflects the surrounding coastal environment and the greens of the Torrey Pines Golf Course. Early California Impressionist art graces the walls and signature restaurant.

Rancho Valencia Resort

MAP E2 ▪ 5921 Valencia Circle, Rancho Santa Fe ▪ (858) 756-1123 ▪ www. ranchovalencia.com ▪ $$$
Bougainvillea cascades over the Spanish casitas in this stunning resort. Many rooms feature cathedral ceilings, private terraces, and fireplaces. Rejuvenation treatments include reflexology, aromatherapy, and various massages.

The Westgate Hotel

MAP J4 1055 Second Avenue ▪ (619) 238-1818 ▪ www.westgatehotel. com ▪ $$$
With a lobby that suggests the anteroom of the Palace of Versailles, complete with Baccarat crystal chandeliers, Persian carpets, and French tapestries, this grand hotel offers good value for its downtown location. Spacious rooms with European decor have views of San Diego.

Heritage and Vintage Hotels

Inn at the Park

MAP C5 ▪ 525 Spruce St ▪ (619) 291-0999 ▪ No air conditioning ▪ No dis. access ▪ www.shell hospitality.com ▪ $
This 1926 inn was popular with Hollywood celebrities en route to their vacations

in Mexico in the 1920s and 1930s. The original fixtures lend a delightful retro touch.

Gaslamp Plaza Suites

MAP K4 ▪ 520 E St ▪ (619) 232-9500 ▪ www. gaslampplaza.com ▪ $$
Now on the National Register of Historic Places, this building still features much of its original 1913 craftsmanship, such as Australian gumwood, Corinthian marble, and an elevator door made of brass. Complimentary breakfast is served on the rooftop terrace.

Glorietta Bay Inn

MAP C6 ▪ 1630 Glorietta Blvd, Coronado ▪ (619) 435-3101 ▪ www. gloriettabayinn.com ▪ $$
Many of the original fixtures of John D. Spreckels' *(see p43)* 1908 Edwardian mansion remain, including the unique hand-made plaster moldings, chandeliers, and a marble staircase. Splurge on one of the antique-filled guest rooms inside the house for a more decadent experience.

The Grande Colonial

MAP N3 ▪ 910 Prospect St, La Jolla ▪ (888) 828-5498 ▪ www.thegrande colonial.com ▪ $$
La Jolla's first hotel was designed by Spanish Revival architect Richard Requa *(see p43)*. The 1913 building houses luxury suites, while a 1926 building contains the main hotel. Elegantly appointed rooms are in keeping with the hotel's European ambience.

Horton Grand Hotel

MAP J5 ▪ 311 Island Ave ▪ (619) 544-1886 ▪ www. hortongrand.com ▪ $$
Rebuilt from two Victorian-era hotels, this hotel reflects the character of the Gaslamp Quarter. Rooms are individually decorated in period style, and each has a gas fireplace.

The Inn at Rancho Santa Fe

MAP E2 ▪ 5951 Linea del Cielo, Rancho Santa Fe ▪ (858) 756-1131 ▪ www. theinnatrsf.com ▪ $$
Refined elegance distinguishes this romantic country inn. Many of the red-roofed adobe casitas scattered about the lush grounds boast comfy queen-sized beds, fireplaces, and kitchens.

The Keating Hotel

MAP K5 ▪ 432 F Street ▪ (619) 814-5700 ▪ www. thekeating.com ▪ $$
Set in a historic 1890 building in the heart of the Gaslamp Quarter, this super-hip boutique hotel was created by the Italian designers responsible for Ferrari and Maserati. The rooms have open rainfall showers.

La Jolla Beach and Tennis Club

MAP N3 ▪ 2000 Spindrift Drive ▪ La Jolla ▪ (858) 412-2036 ▪ www.ljbtc.com ▪ $$$
This resort is perfect for an active family: guests can choose to ocean swim, kayak, play tennis or golf, or simply enjoy the sunshine. You can step out the door onto a pristine sand beach. Rooms with kitchenettes are available.

U.S. Grant

MAP J4 ■ 326 Broadway ■ (619) 232-3121 ■ www.usgrant.net ■ $$$
Ulysses S. Grant Jr. commissioned this stately 1910 Renaissance palace. A $56-million renovation has restored it to its former glory, with mahogany furniture and paneling, tile floors, and luxurious rooms.

La Valencia Hotel

MAP N2 ■ 1132 Prospect St, La Jolla ■ (858) 454-0771 ■ www.lavalencia.com ■ $$$
Since 1926, the "Pink Lady of La Jolla" has enchanted with its splendid Mediterranean ambience, exquisite decor, and ideal location on the cliffs above La Jolla Cove. Rooms vary from quite small to large ocean villas.

Destination Spas

La Costa Resort & Spa

MAP D1 ■ 2100 Costa Del Mar Rd, Carlsbad ■ (760) 438-9111 ■ www.lacosta.com ■ $$
This Spanish-Colonial complex contains two PGA championship golf courses, a tennis center, and the Chopra Center for Wellbeing – a spa and fitness center offering healing treatments.

Cal-a-Vie

MAP D1 ■ 29402 Spa Havens Rd, Vista ■ (760) 842-6831 ■ www.calavie.com ■ $$$
Exhilarating programs focus on fitness, nutrition, and personal care. The Mediterranean-style villas provide luxurious accommodations.

Golden Door

MAP E2 ■ 777 Deer Springs Rd, San Marcos ■ No dis. access ■ (760) 744-5777 ■ www.goldendoor.com ■ $$$
Modeled after the ancient ryokan inns, Japanese gardens, streams, and waterfalls make a glorious backdrop to a week of fitness and meditation. For most of the year, the spa is a women-only domain.

Rancho La Puerta

MAP F3 ■ 476 Tecate Rd, Tecate, Baja California, Mexico ■ (858) 764-5500 ■ www.rancholapuerta.com ■ $$$
Since 1940, guests have pursued body and mind fitness at this beautiful Mexican-Colonial-style resort. Lodgings are in casitas decorated with folk art and bright fabrics. The dining room specializes in homegrown organic food.

Business Hotels

Town & Country Resort & Convention Center

MAP C4 ■ 500 Hotel Circle N. ■ (619) 291-7131 ■ www.towncountry.com ■ $
This sprawling family-owned resort has an onsite convention center and 1,000 rooms. Next door is a golf course, a trolley stop, and the Fashion Valley Mall.

Embassy Suites Hotel San Diego Bay – Downtown

MAP H5 ■ 601 Pacific Hwy ■ (619) 239-2400 ■ www.embassysuites.com ■ $$
Guests enjoy spacious suites that have a living area and a separate bedroom. All rooms open onto a palm-tree-filled atrium and offer a view of the bay or city. Enjoy a dip in the indoor pool.

Hilton La Jolla Torrey Pines

MAP D2 ■ 10950 N. Torrey Pines Rd, La Jolla ■ (858) 558-1500 ■ www.hiltonlajollatorreypines.com ■ $$
This low-key but chic hotel is located next to the Torrey Pines Golf Course. A valet can look after your immediate needs, and a car service is available to drive you to La Jolla. All rooms have balconies or terraces, and many feature ocean or harbor views.

Hyatt Regency La Jolla

MAP B1 ■ 3777 La Jolla Village Dr, La Jolla ■ (858) 552-1234 ■ www.lajolla.hyatt.com ■ $$
Postmodern architect Michael Graves designed this Italian-style palace hotel. A fitness spa and highly acclaimed restaurants are situated next door. Corporate guests can access the business center.

Omni San Diego Hotel

MAP K6 ■ 675 L St ■ (619) 231-6664 ■ www.omnihotels.com ■ $$
A skyway links the hotel to Petco Park, and you can even see the ball field from some rooms. Comfy rooms sport great bathrooms, and if you must tend to business, the Convention Center is only a few blocks away.

Westin San Diego Hotel

MAP H4 ■ 400 W. Broadway ■ (619) 239-4500 ■ www.westinsandiego.com ■ $$
You can't miss this hotel's green silhouette

of hexagonal glass towers. Amenities include ergonomic work chairs and high-speed Internet access. The Convention Center is within easy walking distance.

Manchester Grand Hyatt San Diego

MAP H5 ■ 1 Market Place ■ (619) 232-1234 ■ www.manchester grand.hyatt.com ■ $$$
Two high-rise towers hold 1,625 rooms, many with personal work areas and all with high-speed Internet. The lounge on the 40th floor is one of San Diego's best. Guests can also make use of two rooftop pools and the 24-hour fitness center.

Marriott Marquis San Diego Marina

MAP J6 ■ 333 W. Harbor Dr ■ (619) 234-1500 ■ www.marriotthotels. com ■ $$$
Most rooms at this busy hotel are set up with worktables and high-speed Internet, and offer scenic views of the waterfront and San Diego Bay. The marina and waterfall swimming pool make great distractions.

Westin Gaslamp Quarter San Diego

MAP J4 ■ 910 Broadway Cir ■ (619) 239-2200 ■ www.starwoodhotels. com ■ $$$
Attached to Westfield Horton Plaza, this down-town hotel is close to restaurants and entertain-ment venues. It offers a range of event and meeting spaces, a workout room, and swimming pool. The Gaslamp Quarter and Convention Center are within walking distance.

Moderately Priced Hotels

Bay Club Hotel & Marina

MAP B5 ■ 2131 Shelter Island Dr ■ (619) 224-8888 ■ www.bayclub hotel.com ■ $
Rattan furniture and tropical fabrics give a Polynesian cast to this hotel. The best rooms are at the back and have views of the marina and Point Loma. Breakfast is included.

Crowne Plaza San Diego

MAP Q4 ■ 2270 Hotel Circle N. ■ (619) 297-1101 ■ www. cp-sandiego.com ■ $
In the 1960s, a wave of Polynesian-themed hotels sprang up in the area, and those that survived now have a trendy retro feel to them. The tropical decor still rules the public areas, but the rooms are contem-porary and overlook the pool or nearby golf course.

The Dana on Mission Bay

MAP B4 ■ 1710 W. Mission Bay Dr ■ (619) 222-6440 ■ www.thedana.com ■ $
This hotel is incredibly popular with families. All the water activities of Mission Bay are close by, and the hotel also operates free shuttles to SeaWorld. Tropical landscaping surrounds the grounds, and the swimming pool is a real hit with kids.

Humphrey's Half Moon Inn and Suites

MAP B5 ■ 2303 Shelter Island Dr ■ (619) 224-3411 ■ www.halfmoon inn.com ■ $
Its summer concert series (see p60), tropical landscaping, private marina, and long list of activities make this hotel an ideal choice for those looking for some entertainment. You can pay a little more if you would like a room with a view of the bay.

Best Western Plus Hacienda Hotel Old Town

MAP P5 ■ 4041 Harney St ■ (800) 888-1991 ■ www. bestwestern.com ■ $$
On a hillside overlooking Old Town, this charming hacienda-style hotel offers rooms that have private balconies or look onto a courtyard. Free airport transportation is provided.

Hotel Indigo

MAP K5 ■ 509 9th Ave ■ (619) 727-4000 ■ www. hotelindigo.com ■ $$
Rooms at this trendy, pet-friendly boutique hotel in the Gaslamp Quarter come with plush bedding, hardwood floors, and complimentary Internet access. The bar terrace looks right over Petco Park and has spectacular views of the city skyline.

Waterfront Hotels

Bahia Resort Hotel

MAP A4 ■ 998 W. Mission Bay Dr ■ (858) 488-0551 ■ No dis. access ■ www. bahiahotel.com ■ $
This venerable Mission Bay Hotel is right next to the bay and Mission Beach. Among the facilities on offer are tennis courts, a hydro-therapy pool, and a fitness center. At night, you can enjoy live music on the *Bahia Belle*, a stern-wheeler that floats on the bay every evening.

For a key to hotel price categories see p116

Carlsbad Inn Beach Resort
MAP D1 ■ 3075 Carlsbad Blvd, Carlsbad ■ (760) 434-7020 ■ www.carlsbadinn.com ■ $$
Families really love this sprawling resort. Its rooms and timeshare condominiums are available nightly or weekly. Several activities and classes are held daily, and there is also a good Mexican restaurant.

Catamaran Resort Hotel
MAP A3 ■ 3999 Mission Blvd ■ (858) 488-1081 ■ www.catamaranresort.com ■ $$
This Polynesian-themed hotel offers a long list of water activities. It is within walking distance of many restaurants, and Tiki torches light your way through lushly landscaped grounds. The upper floors of the towers have great views.

Hyatt Regency Mission Bay Spa and Marina
MAP B4 ■ 1441 Quivira Road ■ (619) 224-1234 ■ www.missionbay. regency. hyatt.com ■ $$
This large, family-friendly resort offers pools and water slides, as well as access to a full marina with kayaks, jet-skis, and sailboats. Spacious rooms feature balconies with lovely views of the Pacific, Mission Bay, or the lush gardens.

Pacific Terrace
MAP A3 ■ 610 Diamond St ■ (858) 581-3500 ■ www.pacificterrace.com ■ $$
Sunset views over the Pacific define high living at one of San Diego's finest beach hotels. Large guest rooms come with a balcony or patio. There's no full-service restaurant, but the friendly staff can suggest neighborhood dining options.

Crystal Pier Hotel
MAP A3 ■ 4500 Ocean Blvd ■ (858) 483-6983 ■ No dis. access ■ www.crystalpier.com ■ $$$
Reservations are essential for these 1927 Cape Cod-style cottages that sit directly on the pier. Many have kitchenettes, and patios with views of Pacific Beach.

Tower 23 Hotel
MAP A3 ■ 723 Felspar St, Pacific Beach ■ (877) 648–5738 ■ www.t23hotel.com ■ $$$
Situated on the beach, this stylish hotel features luxury rooms with rain showers, sleek teak furnishings, and high-end amenities. In-room massages are available on request. The classy JRDN restaurant serves delicious authentic Californian seafood.

Bed and Breakfasts

Crone's Cobblestone Cottage B&B
MAP C4 ■ 1302 Washington Place ■ (619) 295-4765 ■ No credit cards ■ No private bathrooms ■ No air conditioning ■ www.cronescobblestonebandb.com ■ $
At this restored 1913 Craftsman-style bungalow, choose either the Elliott or the Eaton room, both furnished with period antiques. The walls are lined with thousands of books.

Hillcrest House
MAP C4 ■ 3845 Front Street ■ 619-990-2441 ■ www.hillcresthousebandb.com ■ $
Choose from five uniquely decorated rooms at this vintage bed and breakfast. It is well situated for San Diego's attractions, and hostess Ann can help you plan your day over a healthy continental breakfast or in the parlor in front of the fireplace.

Julian Gold Rush Hotel
MAP E2 ■ 2032 Main St, Julian ■ (760) 765-0201 ■ No dis. access ■ No air conditioning ■ www.julianhotel.com ■ $
Built in 1897 by a freed slave from Missouri, this quaint inn is the oldest continually operating hotel in Southern California. Its lacy curtains might remind you of your grandma's house, but the breakfasts are exceptional.

The Artists' Loft
MAP E2 ■ Strawberry Hill, Julian ■ (760) 765-0765 ■ No air conditioning ■ www.artistsloft.com ■ $$
Secluded and romantic, three cabins deep in the woods will inspire the artist within you. Airy Craftsman-style interiors feature natural wood, fine textiles, a full kitchen, and a wood-burning stove. From your screened porch, gaze at stunning mountain and distant coastline views.

Hotel Marisol
MAP C6 ■ 1017 Park Place ■ (619) 365-4677 ■ $$
Escape the crowds at this intimate Spanish-style inn, which has hosted

guests since 1927. Guest rooms are decorated in soft colors and have plantation shutters. A continental breakfast is complimentary, as are beach chairs and bicycles. Coronado's famous beach is only 5 minutes away.

The Inn at Europa Village
MAP E1 ▪ 33350 La Serena Way, Temecula ▪ (951) 676-7047 ▪ www. europavillage.com ▪ $$
Ideally situated for touring the Temecula vineyards, rooms in this Mission-style inn have private balconies, Jacuzzis, and fireplaces. Rates include a continental breakfast with fresh pastries.

Orchard Hill Country Inn
MAP F2 ▪ 2502 Washington St, Julian ▪ (760) 765-1700 ▪ www. orchardhill.com ▪ $$
At this most luxurious of Julian's B&B inns, you can stay in a Craftsman-style cottage with a whirlpool tub, fireplace, and private porch. The tasty breakfasts make for a good start to the day.

Budget Hotels and Hostels

Apple Tree Inn
MAP E2 ▪ 4360 Highway 78, Julian ▪ (760) 765-0222 ▪ www.julianapple treeinn.com ▪ $
A few miles outside of Julian, this small cinder-block-style motel offers a quiet night's sleep in basic but tidy rooms that have mountain views and an outdoor pool. Hiking trails, a few restaurants, and shops are nearby. Pet-friendly.

Borrego Springs Motel
MAP F1 ▪ 2376 Borrego Springs Road ▪ (760) 767-4339 ▪ www.borrego springsmotel.com ▪ $
There are seven queen-bed rooms and one twin-bed room in this no-frills but sparkling clean motel – perfect for those who want to enjoy the surrounding desert. Despite solar power, the motel offers no Wi-Fi, TV, or telephones. The helpful proprietors, who live onsite, are local experts.

HI San Diego Downtown Hostel
MAP K5 ▪ 521 Market St ▪ (619) 525-1531 ▪ No dis. access ▪ No air conditioning ▪ No private bathrooms ▪ www.san diegohostels.org ▪ $
This bright hostel offers dorm rooms and some private ones, free airport transportation and breakfast, kitchen and lounge facilities, laundry service, and Internet access.

Kings Inn, Hotel Circle
MAP C4 ▪ 1333 Hotel Circle South ▪ (619) 297-2231 ▪ www.kingsinn sandiego.com ▪ $
This vintage-style inn with a swimming pool and spa tub has clean, comfortable rooms and friendly, helpful staff. Good onsite restaurants serve breakfast, lunch, and dinner.

Old Town Inn
MAP B4 ▪ 4444 Pacific Hwy ▪ (619) 260-8024 ▪ www.oldtown-inn.com ▪ $
The rooms here are clean and comfy, and the hotel offers one of the better

breakfasts around. An efficiency unit comes with a microwave, refrigerator, and range top, and parking is also free.

La Pensione
MAP H3 ▪ 606 W. Date St ▪ (619) 236-8000 ▪ No air conditioning ▪ www. lapensionehotel.com ▪ $
In the heart of Little Italy, La Pensione offers rooms with a queen-size bed, TV, and refrigerator. A coin-operated laundry is on the premises, as well as free parking, and some of the city's best Italian restaurants are just a stone's throw away.

USA Hostels Gaslamp
MAP K5 ▪ 726 5th Ave ▪ (619) 232-3100 ▪ No dis. access ▪ No air conditioning ▪ No private bathrooms ▪ www. usahostels.com ▪ $
A popular centrally located hostel offering dorm rooms and some private rooms. Facilities include Internet access, a laundry, kitchen, a lounge area with DVDs, and free lockers. The place is famous for its all-you-can-make pancake breakfasts.

Vagabond Inn Point Loma
MAP B5 ▪ 1325 Scott St ▪ (619) 224-3371 ▪ www. vagabondinn.com ▪ $
This motel is well situated for sportfishing activities and the Cabrillo National Monument. Along with the clean and cheery rooms, guests can enjoy the free breakfast, airport shuttle, parking, and the huge outdoor swimming pool.

General Index

Acknowledgments

Author

Born in San Diego, Pamela Barrus is an unapologetic vagabond, having traveled solo through some 200 countries. She is the author of *Dream Sleeps: Castle and Palace Hotels of Europe* and has contributed to a number of national magazines. She still finds San Diego one of the best places in the world to come home to and enjoy the sunshine.

The author would like to thank Mary Barrus and Roger Devenyns for sharing their exceptional knowledge and insight of San Diego with her.

Additional contributor
Marael Johnson

Publishing Director Georgina Dee

Publisher Vivien Antwi

Design Director Phil Ormerod

Editorial Michelle Crane, Rachel Fox, Priyanka Kumar, Lucy Richards, Sands Publishing Solutions, Sally Schafer, Sophie Wright

Design Tessa Bindloss, Richard Czapnik, Vinita Venugopal

Commissioned Photography Robert Holmes

Picture Research Sumita Khatwani, Ellen Root, Lucy Sienkowska, Rituraj Singh

Cartography Suresh Kumar, James Macdonald, Rajesh Kumar Mishra, Casper Morris

DTP Jason Little

Production Luca Bazzoli

Factchecker Carolyn Patten

Proofreader Kathryn Glendenning

Indexer Hilary Bird

Picture Credits

The publisher would like to thank the following for their kind permission to reproduce their photographs:

Key: a-above; b-below/bottom; c-centre; f-far; l-left; r-right; t-top

123RF.com: Jon Bilous 1, 4cla; Florian Blümm 10cl; Kan Khampanya 4crb; Stephen Minkler 11tl; Sean Pavone 4b; Scott Prokop 21tr; Wasin Pummarin 7br.

1500 Ocean: 65tr.

Alamy Stock Photo: America 3tr, 10bl, 106-7; Art Directors & TRIP 95cl; Paul Briden 16cla; Citizen of the Planet 34cla, 53cl; Collection Christophel 61tr; Gary Crabbe 56br; Ian G Dagnall 49cl, 77tl, 100cla; David R. Frazier Photolibrary, Inc. 26cr; Danita Delimont 79cl, 94t; f8grapher 16br; GALA Images 10c; Joseph S Giacalone 35tl, 53b, 94clb; Gistimages Guardian of Water by Donal Hord with permission of the County of San Diego 49tr; Granger Collection, NYC. 42b; Ian Dagnall Commercial Collection 12br, 69cra; Blaine Harrington III 23bl; Juice Images 54bl; David Kilpatrick 73br; Elizabeth Leyden 32bc; LH Images 29tl, 71tr; W. G. Murray 63cl; Ron Niebrugge 4clb; George Ostertag 20c, 98tl, 102b; Gino Rigucci 30-1; RooM the Agency 38cl; SeBuKi 55cl; Steve Shuey 39tl; Witold Skrypczak 17crb; Stephen Saks Photography 70t; Sueddeutsche Zeitung Photo 43cl; SuperStock 33tl; Craig Steven Thrasher 93bl; TongRo Images 57cb; Visions from Earth 12-3; Jason O. Watson 57tl; Nik Wheeler 27crb, 32clb; Richard Wong 96cl; ZUMA Press Inc 17cl, 29bc, 73cla, 89cla, 101cl.

AWL Images: Danita Delimont Stock 2tl, 8-9.

Balboa Park Conservancy: 46tl.

Balboa Theatre: Brady Architectural Photography 13cr.

Belly Up Tavern: Pixel Perfect Images/ Daniel Knighton 104t.

Belmont Park: 34-5, 59b.

Bertrand at Mr. A's: 64t.

Cafe Sevilla: 62br.

The Cottage: 67tr.

Crest Cafe: 89cb.

Del Mar Rendezvous: 105ca.

Dreamstime.com: Adeliepenguin 18-9, 36-7, 50tl, 100-1; Agezinder 48bl; Alysta 48tr; Americanspirit 93tr; Joe Avery 56tl; Rinus Baak 78tl; Jay Beiler 32-3; Jon Bilous 3tl, 74-5, 90-1; Bshel1983 21cl; Scott Burns 33crb; Chicco7 58tl; Alan Crosthwaite 28cb; Kobby Dagan 18crb, 72bl; Dobino 72c; Durson Services Inc. 11cr; F11photo 10cla, 82crb; F8grapher 68bl; James Feliciano 37crb; Ben Graham 31cr, 52tl; Jorg Hackemann 15crb; Irina88w 84tr, 86cl; Ritu Jethani 19crb, 88clb; Kongomonkey 7tl, 44cla; Meunierd 77crb; Stephen Minkler 42ca; Petthomas 14-5; Photoquest 50bl; Razyph 72tr; Gino Rigucci 92ca; Sonyavraykova 37tl; Stasvolik 54tr; Steveheap 44br; Mirko Vitali 51tr; Angie Westre 55br; Zhukovsky 21br.

Eddie V's Prime Seafood: 65clb.

The Field Irish Pub: 66b.

Getty Images: Davel5957 4cl; Blaine Harrington III 4t; Mark Whitt Photography 99b; Stephen Saks 38bl; Maureen P Sullivan 34bc; Rob Tilley 4cr.

Hotel Del Coronado: 28-9.

Humphrey's Concerts by the Bay: 60b.

iStockphoto.com: Siestacia 85cr; Ron Thomas 11cra, 11crb, 11b, 15tc, 24-5, 30br, 38-9, 86-7; Tobiasjo 30cl; Art Wager 82tl.

La Jolla Playhouse: Kevin Berne 36bl; Joan Marcus 2tr, Sutton Foster (center) and the cast of La Jolla Playhouse's Tony Award-winning production of, THOROUGHLY MODERN MILLIE 40-1.

Lestat's Coffee House: 66ca.

Lou & Mickey's: 83cr.

Manchester Grand Hyatt: 67cl.

Marie Hitchcock Puppet Theatre: 58crb.

Maritime Museum of San Diego: 47cla.

Miguel's Cocina: 97b.

Mille Fleurs: 105crb.

Museum of Man: 76tl.

Museum of Photographic Arts: RyanGobuty Gensler 81cr.

The Old Globe: 60cla.

Photoshot: 13tl; Nikhilesh Haval 27cl.

Prohibition: 62tl.

Putnam Foundation, Timken Museum of Art, San Diego: 70bc.

Reuben H. Fleet Science Center: 18cla, 59tl.

Rex by Shutterstock: Everett Collection 43tr; Zhao Hanrong 20t.

San Diego Automotive Museum: 23c.

San Diego Botanic Garden: 103cla.

San Diego Museum of Art: 22clb, 81tl.

San Diego Natural History Museum: 22tr.

Seaport Village: 14br, 69b.

Spanish Village Art Center: 47b.

Spin: 63tr.

Spreckels Organ Pavilion: Robert Lang 71cl.

Spreckels Theatre: 61cl.

SuperStock: AGE Fotostock/George Ostertag 51cl; Richard Cummins 45br; George Ostertag 99cra.

Vocabulary: 80b.

Cover

Front and spine: **Alamy Stock Photo:** Johnny Stockshooter.

Back: **Dreamstime.com:** Photoquest.

Pull Out Map Cover

Alamy Stock Photo: Johnny Stockshooter.

All other images © Dorling Kindersley

For further information see:
www.dkimages.com

As a guide to abbreviations in visitor information blocks: **Adm** = admission charge; **DA** = disabled access; **D** = dinner; **L** = lunch.

Penguin Random House

Printed and bound in China

First published in Great Britain in 2005 by Dorling Kindersley Limited 80 Strand, London WC2R 0RL

Copyright 2005, 2017 © Dorling Kindersley Limited

A Penguin Random House Company

17 18 19 20 10 9 8 7 6 5 4 3 2 1

Reprinted with revisions 2007, 2009, 2011, 2013, 2017

ISBN 978 0 2412 7638 9

MIX
Paper from responsible sources
FSC™ C018179
www.fsc.org

Street Index